SHAKING THE TREE

brazen. short. memoir.

Edited by Marni Freedman & Tracy J. Jones

Published by MCM Publishing
9880 Shadow Road
San Diego, CA 91941
www.mcmpublishing.com

Editors: Marni Freedman & Tracy J. Jones
Assistant editor: Danielle B. Baldwin
Copyeditor: Erin Willard
Book cover and interior design by Monkey C Media, www.monkeyCmedia.com

First edition
Printed in the United States of America

ISBN (paperback): 978-0-9974413-6-9
ISBN (eBook): 978-0-9974413-7-6

LCCN: 2018954439

To those seeking the courage
to tell their stories:
welcome to the tribe.
Your messy, complicated,
glorious story matters.

Dear Reader,

Many of these stories were born in everyday writing workshops. They were brought in as homework assignments. We, as the teachers of memoir, marveled week after week at the spectacular moments of life—sometimes ordinary—sometimes extraordinary—hidden within these writer's souls, often for decades.

There came a time when we could no longer sit still. The stories were so vivid, so powerful that an idea was born. Take these remarkable stories and give them a voice through an actor on the stage.

For three years, we've had the honor of bringing these stories to life in a Memoir Showcase, which matched the top stories with a professional actor, editor, director, and theater. What we launched as a one-time-experiment has taken on a life of its own and become one of San Diego's premiere memoir programs giving breath to true and compelling stories.

Audiences were gripped by the unique intimacy of glimpsing into the pivotal moments of another's life. The actors, directors, and storytellers were changed forever. We, as editors of this anthology, have culled the top pieces that were either submitted to our annual competition or performed on stage. As our last program said, "You can't make this stuff up."

We hope you dive into these pages, see yourself reflected within them, and feel touched in a way that only memoir can.

Sincerely,
Marni and Tracy

Shaking the Tree, Vol. 1, 2018

brazen. short. memoir

NO WAY BACK

MAHSHID FASHANDI HAGER

PART 1

I'm six years old and there's a revolution outside my front door.

It screams and shouts and pours itself onto the streets of Tehran.

I hear it at night, see signs of it in the morning:

broken glass, burnt trash cans, burnt cars

Fear, like a big, dark blanket, covers my whole house.

My dad's late coming home and I'm scared. "Don't be scared," Mom says. "He's safe at work. Be brave."

He might be arrested or maybe shot. He might never come home.

I hide and wait and hold my breath until he finally does. He finds me and as he lifts me up in his arms, fear lifts up and floats away too.

He doesn't know it yet, but it's about to get worse.

I'm seven years old and a big sister now. The king of Iran is gone. His family too.

I see on the news how his friends are killed every day: Men in blindfolds, shot against the wall, or hanging from cranes.

Mom says I can't play outside anymore.

I must wear the hijab, and I hate it. It's too hot. It slips off and I get in trouble.

There's afternoon prayer at school and Mom says I have to do it, but I don't know how.

"Just pretend," she says. "You're safe at school."

She doesn't know it yet, but it's about to get worse.

I'm eight years old and have two sisters. Nobody goes outside to play.

There are so many rules: "Don't talk to strangers. Don't forget your hijab.

"Don't listen to music. Don't dance. Don't make eye contact."

Mom and Dad whisper and think I can't hear. They're worried and think I don't know.

They think they're fooling me. "You're safe at home. Be brave."

They don't know it yet, but it's about to get worse.

I'm nine years old and we are at war with Iraq.

There are lines for everything: lines for bread and chicken. Lines for milk and diapers and gas. The lights go out at night. We eat dinner by candlelight and wait for the sirens we know will come. When they do, we rush down to the cellar.

I cover my ears and bury my head in my mom's lap. But I still hear them.

The explosions, some far away, some closer, rattle the ground and shake me to my core.

We don't know it yet, but it's about to get worse.

I'm ten years old and soldiers are in my house, soldiers with guns, yelling at us to leave, leave now.

They say the house that shares our backyard wall is occupied by the mujahidin and they're going to blow it up.

Mom wants to call Dad but there's no time.

Our neighbor across the street takes us in.

We hear shots and screams, explosions and glass breaking.

The roads are blocked and Dad takes a long time to come.

The fighting continues all night long. Dad holds Mom while she cries.

I wake up to daylight and silence.

Dad says, "You're going to school." I want to protest, but I don't.

He takes my hand and we go outside.

There are bullet shells on the ground, curtains hanging from tree branches, soldiers inside our house, glass shards everywhere.

Dad picks me up and covers my eyes, but it's too late.

I've seen the bodies out on the front porch, covered with our sheets.

Dad helps me get ready, puts me on the bus, and waves goodbye.

I want to scream, but I don't. I pretend to be brave.

That night, our house is on the news. Our yard, our kitchen, our sheets covering bodies.

The soldiers celebrating.

PART 2

Three weeks later there's a smuggler in our living room.

Ali, Ali of the Mountains. He says we can get away to Turkey.

He says one bag and I look around my room. My favorite pillow. My favorite dress. My favorite doll. He says, "no goodbyes," and I think of my best friend.

When Mom talks to her mother one last time on the phone, she covers the receiver so Grandma won't hear her cry.

A few days later, we board a bus at midnight.

"Where are we going?" I ask. "How long 'til we get there?

"Will it be better where we are going? Will we ever come back?"

So many questions without answers. "It'll be a long journey," Dad says. "Go to sleep."

I wake with a jolt. We are stopped at a checkpoint.

Soldiers with guns enter the bus.

Wide-eyed, Mom grabs me by the shoulders.

"Remember, we're going to visit your uncle in Tabriz," she says. "We're only staying a few days."

The soldiers talk to some passengers and search the bus, but they leave empty-handed.

Back on the road, I look at Dad and his smile says, "We tricked them. We're brave!"

So, I pretend too—it's all a big game, we'll be home soon.

When we arrive in Tabriz, I wake up to find I've wet myself.

I don't know when or how. I cry and tell Mom.

She helps me clean up and change into my only other pants. She says: "It's okay. It happens," but we both know it isn't supposed to.

The next morning, we're loaded into a truck.

Dad is up front with the driver and I wish I could sit with him.

He explains we're trying to get closer to the border with Turkey.

As we drive in silence over bumpy dirt roads, I try to imagine what the border will look like, what Turkey will look like, what safety will feel like.

Awakening from restless sleep, I hear the driver cursing under his breath.

There's another checkpoint up ahead. Dad says it's okay, but I know he is scared.

We stop as men with rifles slung around their shoulders approach the car.

Words are exchanged in loud, angry voices, words that I don't understand, ringing in my ears.

Dad looks at us in the back seat, saying something I can't hear.

Someone kicks the car and our driver accelerates, trying to escape.

More men with guns approach. I hear the words "Traitors! Shoot them!"

A rifle is drawn, pointed at my dad.

Mom wraps a free arm around my head and pulls me into her chest.

I can't see. I can't move. I can't breathe.

And then … it all stops. I hear crying, my mother, my sisters.

Dad is standing outside, talking to the man who almost killed him. I don't understand.

"It's okay," Mom says through tears. "Just a misunderstanding."

But I still don't understand.

The driver returns to the truck. Dad doesn't.

Without him, we're driven up the road to a house where women make us tea and try to console my mom. But she can't stop crying.

We wait and wait for my father. Half an hour? Three hours? I don't know.

I try not make a sound. I try not to move a muscle. I just wait.

The women set up the room for lunch and men arrive, one by one or in groups of two or three—all with guns. I've never seen so many guns.

I look at their faces and ask silently, "Is my dad alive? Did you kill him? Are we next?"

Then I hear my dad, talking to someone. It's Ali!

Relief washes over my whole body and I can breathe again.

We eat chicken, eggs and goat cheese, yogurt and bread.

We don't know it yet, but this will be our last warm meal for a while.

I slowly begin to understand.

These men with guns will guide us through the mountains.

They will show us the way. We must trust them.

Everything in me is screaming no, but I have to be brave.

As dusk approaches, we load mules with our bags and blankets, water and bread.

And as the night sky starts to spread over the mountains, we begin to walk.

PART 3

We walk for hours through snow and mud.

We walk until I can't feel my feet.

We walk until all I can think about is *not* walking.

Sometime in the still of the night we reach a small stone hut. Inside, we drop to the dirt ground and pass out without saying a word.

I wake up, trying to get up, but my legs fail me.

I want to go outside, but Dad says we can't.

"Helicopters are out searching the area for refugees this morning." He says, "We must hide inside."

Mom rocks my sisters, comforting them. Dad paces. Four steps forward, four steps back.

When the helicopters leave and darkness falls, we walk again.

The trail becomes more treacherous.

I slip and fall, over and over again. The mules are slipping too.

Ali says the guides are going to walk the mules back. This is as far as they go.

He will run ahead a bit to see if we should go on tonight.

"You stay here," he says. "I'll come back for you."

I try to follow him with my eyes, but darkness swallows him after a few steps.

While he's gone, the men rob us at gunpoint.

It's not a big scene. They have guns, we don't. They're strong, we're not.

They know the way and we don't.

They pat us down, looking for money. They rob us of our last possessions and leave.

We are left behind, and I'm sure we'll die here.

I watch my dad cry and I hear my heart breaking. "No way back now," he says.

When Ali gets back, he doesn't ask, and we don't tell. We just walk.

Every muscle in my body hurts.

"A little while longer," Ali says. He says this all the time.

Despite being carried on Dad's and Ali's shoulders, my sisters are tired of this "adventure."

They cry and they fuss and I wish they would stop.

"What's your favorite movie?" Ali asks my sister over his shoulder.

"*The Sound of Music*," my sister answers.

"What do you like about it?"

"The songs."

"Teach me the songs."

"Raindrops on roses and whiskers on kittens."

Her voice echoes in the mountains.

"Bright copper kettles and warm woolen mittens."

"This is a great song!" Ali says. My sister giggles.

"Brown paper packages tied up with strings." She gets louder and louder.

"These are a few of my favorite things."

She continues singing. I look at my dad and he's smiling for the first time in a long time. We all pick up our pace a little. And for the next few moments we pretend we're in the movie.

This moment will carry me through the next few days.

I don't know it yet, but it will carry me through months and years to come.

Every time I think we're close, Ali points at another mountain we need to climb. It's been too dangerous and too challenging and Ali pretends he told us so. I hate him and fear him, yet I know we'd be dead without him.

Four days, five, six—I lose track of time as day turns to night and night turns to day. Nights that are the darkest shade of black. I can't make out the shape of those walking right in front of me.

I can just hear their breath, heavy and strained.

Then, I hear Mom whimpering. She sits and refuses to walk any further. "This was a mistake," she says. "Just leave me here." Ali puts her hand into mine, looks me in the eye and says, "Make sure she keeps moving."

I'm hungry but I walk. I'm hurt and cold and scared, but I walk. I don't cry or complain. I don't talk. I just walk. And now I make sure Mom walks too.

I don't feel like I'm ten anymore.

And then out of the darkness, I see lights, flickering like candles—so far away and small, I wonder if I've imagined them.

Some part of my tired, beaten brain warns me that it's danger—fire, wolves' eyes! Hungry wolves, waiting for us. I feel tears running down my face.

But as we get closer, I can see it's not a fire or wolves. It is a house.

A single house. With electricity. With people inside.

A man who's been expecting us opens the door and greets Ali.

He turns to us with a smile and says, "Welcome to Turkey."

My Iran is gone, its replacement behind me.

I don't know it yet, but I'll never go back home.

It's hard to know what lays ahead.

But I'll be brave and I'll keep walking.

STORIES FOR MY FATHER

ANASTASIA ZADEIK

"Get me my red planner, will you?" my father said, motioning toward a white canvas *New Yorker* bag sitting on the window ledge of his hospital room. "I need to check something."

My father never went anywhere without his red planner. Lying there with his gut stapled and stitched together six days after major abdominal surgery, he was holding his iPhone and a stylus, navigating through emails that had piled up while he'd been pumped with opioids. And he had dates to confirm: weddings he was set to perform, plays or operas for which he had season tickets.

"Sweetie?" he added, since I wasn't moving fast enough. Even then, loaded with Percocet, Dad was able to think faster and better than most people I know on their best day. Sitting on his bedside tray were the current *Sports Illustrated*, the latest book about the provenance of certain of Shakespeare's plays, and that day's *Chicago Tribune* crossword, which he'd completed in ink.

It wasn't easy to be my father's daughter. He was a demanding man—of himself and of those around him. High expectations were the only kind. One of my family stories relates how, as the superintendent of my high school, he was asked to speak at the ceremony inducting new members to the National Honor Society. He famously ended his speech with something along the lines of [this is paraphrased] "the young people in this room are destined to do great things. One of you may discover a new treatment for cancer, become a Supreme Court justice or even the president of the United States … and when you get there, sweetie, I hope you remember your dear old dad."

He got the laugh he was looking for; the thing is, he wasn't kidding.

Cancer curer. Supreme Court justice. President.

I did not achieve any of the above.

There is another story that has become lore inside our family. About a year after I graduated from college, *summa cum laude*, Phi Beta Kappa, which garnered a simple, downplayed, "of course she did" from my father, I decided I didn't want to pursue law school as originally planned. I broke this news to my parents at lunch, out, where reactions would be, by necessity, subdued. My father had had a few drinks. My mom and I, iced tea. After I explained my decision, my father said [this is not paraphrased as I will regrettably never forget a word], "I give up on you."

This taught me two important lessons: (1) be careful what you say to your children—a parent's words have the power to build and to inspire … and to crush; and (2) it's not a good idea to live your life for someone else.

At age fifty-three, I am still trying to take these lessons on board; particularly the last one.

The fourth of five children born in rapid succession, I learned early that it was critical to develop something unique to stand out; a five-year-old's decision to be the good girl grew and morphed into life-long perfectionism that hurts. About a year into my first serious therapy, I was given a book to read called *Too Perfect.* I couldn't get through it, which I rationalized as healthy; after all, trying to be better at not being perfect is its own form of being more perfect, isn't it? The one thing I gleaned from the book was how my perfectionism was the direct result of efforts to get the attention from my parents and siblings I so desperately craved.

Attention-seeking I've never grown out of, for they were then (and remain) a marvelous group of people. Basking in their glow was (and is) a phenomenal experience, even if only for a few moments.

My oldest brother, Phil, is smart, athletic, good-looking and clever. Clever in an endearing, funny, quick-witted way. Phil was the bestower of nicknames, the one who knew how to defuse any uncomfortable situation with a pithy comment, and the announcer during family football games or croquet tournaments. "The quarterback goes back for a pass," he'd say as he maneuvered in to tackle me, "she sees the receiver, but, out of nowhere, she's taken down by the defensive back who's just too good." Like my father, Phil is off-the-charts intelligent. A biochemistry major, he took both the MCAT and the LSAT before deciding to go to law school. He was also an excellent dispenser of advice; it was Phil who told me not to go to law school to please our father. "It's bloody hard," he told me. "Only go if you want to be there."

He was a tough act to follow. But follow him we all did.

Amy is second in line. Also smart, outgoing, spunky, and the apple of my father's eye, she was the one that laid the groundwork for her sisters; she fought the good fight for our right to shave our legs, pierce our ears, and stay out on a date past 9:30. At age twelve when I got my period, my mother was out of town, trying to prevent my crazy uncle from doing something crazy, so it was Amy who sat outside the bathroom door, patiently explaining how tampons worked. It was Amy who flew out to meet my newly divorced guy and his one-year-old daughter and give me her blessing, adding a lesson about the necessity of clean hand towels in the guest bathroom. She is, to this day, my go-to person in an emergency or when I just need a friend.

Tricia, the middle girl and middle child, is the brilliantly creative one, the rebel, the one who went to school with wet hair when I was getting up at 6:00 a.m. to create perfect blond Farrah Fawcett curls. Tricia and I shared a room until I was sixteen; we went from taping a line down the middle of our bedroom to whispering in the dark until we were too tired to speak. We shared clothes and hair products and tanning supplies. She and I never have a phone conversation shorter than an hour because she is the only member of my family that tells longer stories than I do. She listens when I have an anxiety attack because I've made the most dreadful mistake, and I do the same for her. She lets me know I'll be okay, no matter what.

My little brother Michael followed me by thirteen months, a rambunctious, too smart for his own good, sweet curly-haired little boy that for many years was like a twin to me. "The oolie-pools," my mother dubbed us, based on a song she used to sing to us in the car when we were tired and cranky and she still had errands to run or children to pick up from school. The song had only one lyric: "Oolie-poolie, oolie-poolie, oolie-poolie"—you get the idea. Only when we were adults did we realize the melody was a college fight song. All that time, we were convinced our mother made it up. Michael grew up to be the uncle that held his nephews and nieces upside down too long; the one my four-year-old son requested as a godfather; the one who gave that same son of mine, when he went off to college, the sage advice, "Don't wake and bake."

Tying us all together was my mother, whose grace, down-to-earth elegance, wisdom and love I cannot begin to explain in words. My father had two nicknames for her: "Swifty," because she was always late, which was likely because of the five-kids-in-quick-succession thing, and "Saint Esther," because she was the closest thing to a perfectly giving human being you can get. My father, my siblings, and I were all the luckiest human beings for living within her orbit. She was the one who comforted us, and who taught us in ways small and large how to be decent, kind, generous, and forgiving. She gave us confidence to rise to the challenges our father posed for us.

After the "I give up on you" comment, I struggled for years to come to terms with having disappointed my father in the most egregious way. I had a career in neuropsychological research, but I didn't cure anything. I raised two children overseas but did not become a lawyer, Supreme Court justice or president of the United States. However, several years ago, before my mother died of Alzheimer's, when we were all losing our center of gravity, I wrote down stories of my rose-colored childhood to share with my father: How we all got our Phil nicknames. The Christmas when all the decorations and gifts were homemade, or the one when my father taught us all to cross-country ski. The time I stole Dad's tape recorder to sing "Hey Jude" over one of his tapes because my fourth-grade teacher told us we didn't sound the way we thought we did and then Dad played the tape during a critically important meeting. The time Tricia and I put Mom on a diet so she could fit into Amy's prom dress for a gala dinner. How I learned to tell stories at our dinner table during my allotted three minutes of "tell the most important thing that happened to you."

I stapled these stories together and gave them to my father for his birthday seven years before he went into the hospital to have his cancerous bladder removed. I did not know how he felt about them until I found them, that day in the hospital, in his *New Yorker* bag, next to his red planner. I stared at the stapled sheaf without removing them from the bag, then turned and met my father's gaze.

"I love those stories," was all he said.

And it was enough.

HARLEM IN HAVANA

JOHN CUNNINGHAM

As a kid, when asked, "Where you from?" I'd proudly say, "Harlem in Havana, Sleeper Car Number Sixty-Six, care of Royal American Shows." And when they asked my name, "Johnny Cunningham, Boobie Bates, Jr." The only thing I knew about my father, Johnny Cunningham, was that he was a dancer and left before I was born. I was given the nickname Boobie, short for booby trap, because I was always getting into trouble, and Bates was Momma's maiden name.

Long before there was a Six Flags America or a Busch Gardens, there was the Royal American Shows, "the World's Largest Midway" and my home for the first ten years of my life, during the 1940s. Based in Tampa, Florida, Royal American, "the Show" for short, played major state fairs and exhibitions from Florida to Oklahoma, Louisiana to Minnesota, and Alberta to Ontario, Canada. Because we lived a nomadic lifestyle, whatever fairground, midway or lot we set up on became our temporary home.

Leon and Gwen Claxton, my aunt and uncle, owned, produced, and performed in an all-black musical revue called "Harlem in Havana," one of the Show's main attractions. Harlem, a Vegas-style show, featured a ten-piece band, dancers, singers, and comedians, and some of the top black acts of the day. My momma was the lead dancer and choreographer with Harlem's troupe.

Uncle Leon could be an ass with a bullish personality one moment, and a suave, happy-go-lucky showman the next. He was also a shrewd, successful businessman who ruled his world with an iron fist, and his Jekyll-and-Hyde personality carried over to his family as well. He and Aunt Gwen were more business partners than a couple, and he treated my cousins like shit. He treated me like a welfare case. But mostly, I was indifferent to Uncle Leon and glad to be under Momma's and Aunt Gwen's protection.

Traveling on the carnival circuit wasn't as glamorous as some of the young entertainers thought it would be. Unless, of course, working in some of the harshest conditions known to show business and not having a "pot to piss in" was glamorous. Traveling the rails, eating cold Spam, and living in crowded quarters was fine by me. I was born into carnival life. For most of Harlem's troupe, the sacrifices were worth it, as Harlem was one of only a few showcases in the country where black entertainers could display their talents. They also got the opportunity to work and train under Uncle Leon, who was one of the best stage managers and chorus-line trainers in the business.

I loved watching the setup and teardown of the tent city. It was magic in motion, an organized chaos that could miraculously turn a dirt lot into a place of beauty and wonder. Once the wagons and rides were pulled off the flat cars and staged on the lot, the seven power units that provided power and lights for the midway were fired up. The lot came alive with the sounds of tractors pulling wagons into place and cadence callers leading the rhythmic pounding of sledgehammers as they drove tent stakes.

Harlem's tent seated one thousand people and housed a full stage, three dressing wagons, and the bally front.

I loved watching the show from the stage wings. I could watch it night after night and never be bored. In front of the stage, it was always the same. But from backstage, you could see the mistakes, the laughter, and the jokes between the entertainers. I played my air drums right along with the band. I didn't have swings or slides to play with, so when I tired of hanging around the tent, I'd climb the tent poles, swing on the guylines and ropes, slide down the canvas tent walls, or go hang out on the midway.

An average day for Harlem's troupe began around 9:00 a.m. with breakfast and rehearsal, then makeup and readying for the first show of the day. Everyone needed to be ready to go by the first "bally" call. Bally, taken from "ballyhoo," is a loud, attention-getting spiel given by a talker or pitchman out in front of the tent to entice the crowd into buying a ticket. All backstage, you could hear Uncle Leon going between the dressing wagons hollering, "Bally, it's bally time!" He also worked the bally stage on occasions when our regular talker, Tony Paradise, was not there.

The talker would put on a show out front with the band playing and the dancers wearing their most revealing costumes, dancing and swaying with the music. Uncle Leon was good, but Tony Paradise was one of the best in the business. You could hear him bellowing all over the midway, "Hurry, hurry, hurry, come on down folks, move in real close now, cause I'm gonna put on a show for you. Look at what you're gonna see inside. Hurry, hurry, hurry, ladies and gents, it's showtime at Harlem in Havana!"

In earlier years, black shows, including Harlem in Havana, were known as "jig" or "minstrel" shows. Racism was not an "in-your-face" problem on the Show, but there was a caste system.

Owners, operators, managers, and entertainers considered themselves "showmen." People who ran the different games, souvenir, and food stands, were "jointys." "Carneys" were everyone else—ride jockeys, tent hands, and the permanent roustabouts. Was there segregation? Sure there was. There were no "Whites Only" signs, but you just knew. The placement of our car, #66, in the train's lineup also screamed, SEGREGATED. The small dining car, nicknamed the "pie car," was placed at the front of the train between Harlem's car and the other carnival cars. This kept Harlem's people from having to transit the rest of the train to get to the pie car, and even at that, they couldn't sit down; it was carryout.

I always ate breakfast in the pie car. Jack, Harlem's tent boss, would save me a seat. "Hey Boobie, come on over here and sit by old Jack." He had this West Texas drawl that reminded me of my grandpa. "So what are we eating this morning; hotcakes or grits?" Whatever I said, he'd order the same, with two eggs over easy. He didn't have a lot to say and wasn't the friendliest of people, but I guess he had a soft spot for me. But on the midway he was all business, yelling, "Goddammit Boobie, get off my canvas! You better leave my ropes alone!"

The Show rolled on ninety train cars. It was truly a sight to see, with its bright red, yellow, black, and silver paint and "Royal American Shows" emblazoned in large letters on the sides of each car. I slept with Momma most nights and spent my days with my cousins. We'd play games and stare out the windows, waving at the locals as we passed through small towns. We couldn't do that when we traveled in the South. In some places, we were warned to keep the windows closed and the shades down. Otherwise, the racist shits would throw rocks and call us things like "niggers," "coons," and "little black Sambo."

I never saw any confrontations between Uncle Leon and Momma. They were cordial yet distant, but it wasn't until his death in 1967 that I found out why. Right after my birthday, in November, I received a letter from Momma that read as follows:

Dear Boobie:

Leon passed away yesterday. Gwen wants you to come home for the funeral; she will send you a ticket. You know I love you very much, my Seed, and would never do or say anything to hurt you, but after giving prayerful consideration to what I'm about to tell you, I know now I should have told you a long time ago.

Leon wasn't just your uncle; he was also your father.

Please forgive me for not telling you sooner, but I promised Gwen to keep it to myself until his death. When I first went on the Show, he raped me. When I turned up pregnant, he paid a dancer, Cunningham, to say he was your father; that's why you have his name. It breaks my heart to have to tell you this. Please forgive me. Give Gwen a call so she can set up your tickets and we can talk when you get here. I love you with all my heart.

Starring Soon, Love Momma.

I was numb and angry. Angry for the lie we had been living all those years. I was denied my own truth and the closeness of a brother and sisters. I wasn't mad at Momma but furious at what Leon had done.

At the end of the Canadian run in 1949, Momma left her boyfriend, the Show, and everything she knew, and we headed for the West Coast and a new life. Momma never looked back, but during the summer of 1958, I got a chance to go back on the road with the Show, back home, one last time. I was seventeen then and longed for the old days.

I never forgot the smell of fresh sawdust, cotton candy, and grilled burgers and onions wafting over the midway. The sounds of the whistles, bells, and bumper cars, and the laughter and screams that came from the old Funhouse, filled my memories. I could still hear Tony Paradise yelling, "Hurry, hurry, hurry! Step right up! It's Harlem in Havana time, and the show's about to start."

It is said, one never forgets home; so I guess Harlem in Havana, Sleeper Car Number Sixty-Six, care of Royal American Shows, really is where I'm from.

HELSINKI, NOVEMBER 1990

JUDY REEVES

Tuesday is Ladies Day at the George Street Baths. It's cold in Helsinki as Camille and I walk the downtown streets, me grateful for my blue Greek coat, lavender Swedish mittens, and white Canadian mukluks. We've stashed oils and lotions and shampoos in our packs. I don't know what to expect at the baths, but I've learned it doesn't much matter what you expect; life—and death—will ultimately have their way with you anyhow.

I've been traveling alone for four months. One of those "sell everything, get an around-the-world airline ticket, pack a single suitcase" kind of journeys you sometimes have to make when your husband has died, and you can't stay home and you don't know where to go, so you set out on an odyssey to either find yourself or to escape the grief. Now, after four months of single rooms and solitude, I've found myself in Helsinki for a rendezvous with my best friend, Camille.

It was our Finnish friend Jorma who told us about the baths. "Go, go. You will love," he said. And so we go, go, to the George Street Swimming Hall—*Yrjönkadun uimahalli*—the oldest public swimming hall in Finland.

Swimming: nude. Sauna: nude. Massage: nude.

Though I've done some of each, I've never done them all together and never with a group of strangers. I'm both shy and excited for the experience, like making love with someone for the first time.

We enter the hall through great wooden doors. The air is warm and humid and smells of chlorine, and for an instant I'm taken back to the indoor pool at the YWCA in San Diego where I sometimes swam as a girl. We always wore swimsuits at the Y, and I'd never even heard of a sauna. Massage was something foreign, too, something they did in Sweden.

Inside the George Street Baths, massive globes glow like full moons above the clear turquoise pool. A balcony rises above the pool with arched openings guarded by graceful, curved wrought iron. Many closed doors line up along the level of the pool. I don't know where these doors lead, and I imagine assignations, rendezvous, afternoon delights, a private session with a masseuse, perhaps. Who knows what pleasures the Finns during their long, dark winters.

Camille and I get our lockers, get out of our clothes, and join the others in the sauna—cedar-scented, dimly lit, dry and warm. We find our place among the six or eight older women who lounge on tiers of wooden benches that rise two and three high in a rectangle around a charcoal burner where hot coals smolder. Just a glance around tells me we are, by far, the youngest of the women gathered here; I celebrated my forty-eighth birthday the month before, alone and lonely and in Greece. Camille is seventeen years my junior. She's a sturdy young woman with bottle-green eyes and a head of curly hair soft as a kitten's fur. I've missed being with her, especially the silliness and laughter. I haven't laughed much during my self-exile; god knows I haven't been silly. I sometimes wonder if I've lost that, too; a light-hearted, easy-to-laugh way of being in the world.

"What are you thinking, Jude?" Camille asks. Good friend that she is, she knows when I've disappeared too far into my thoughts. My husband used to just say, "Penny?" to bring me present again.

"You know," I answer, and she probably does. She's been on the receiving end of my long and wandering and wondering letters of the last four months. Besides, I know anyone can just look at me and see the loss layered underneath it all. Even that woman in Greece, the one who cut my hair, looked at me in the mirror and said, "Your eyes, *tóso lypiró*—so sad."

Scattered around the sauna in twos and threes, the beautifully wrinkled and gray-haired Finnish women sit on their small paper squares, so casual and easy in their bodies. I don't stare; I know the protocol. Still, who doesn't take a surreptitious peek? Seated highest on the tier, one woman, bone-thin, so fragile-looking you think she might shatter at a touch. Her breasts only a dark hint of nipple low on her chest. Another, round in that fairytale grandmother way, like my own grandmother before she died, the same sparse gray hair pulled in a bun, the same arms loose at the underside, what I try to hide with sleeves and shawls. And here they are, these two women, like the half-dozen others in the sauna—the cellulous, the sagging, the softly folding—all with such an open ease about them.

Maybe it's their quiet influence, or maybe the intimate warmth of the small space, the muted light, but I'm soon able to relax. My body loves the hot dry air of the sauna, the cedar smell that wraps around me and enters with each breath. "Let the soft animal of your body love what it loves," the poet Mary Oliver tells us. And mine loves resting naked on the wooden benches, feeling the heat beneath my thighs, across my stomach and breasts. After a while, someone senses the air's longing for moisture and tosses a ladleful of water dipped from a copper pot onto the hot coals. A wet sizzle, a billow of steam, and a minute rise of humidity. But it lasts for just that long, and soon the air resumes its hot and dry and cedar-scented healing.

Among the women—Camille and I, too—conversations are muted. The mind goes liquid. Tension melts from the body. There is only presence and breathing, an occasional murmured sigh.

And then the body says "enough." And you listen, because naked in the sauna you can't help but listen to the body.

Just outside the sauna, the humid, chlorinated air of the pool fills the hall. Turquoise water ripples under haloed lights. I step down into the blue. I can almost hear a slight sizzle as the cool water splashes against my body.

I enter slowly, step by step, holding my arms out to my sides, pulling my stomach muscles tight against the anticipated chill. I like the incremental entry into the womb of water, the way it gradually assumes my body, slicking the back of my knees and the tender skin inside my thighs, startling with its first wet touch against the soft folds of my labia. After the sauna, entering the pool this way is like foreplay. Or maybe the sauna itself is foreplay and entering the pool, the next sensual experience. Falling forward, I surrender to the buoyant blue, letting the water hold me, weightless, as I float, face down, arms outstretched, and then, with held breath, dive under, completely immersed in the cool water as much as, minutes before, I had been immersed in the hot breath of the sauna.

My body is coming alive in a different way, responding to these new sensations. Rather than softly humming, it's singing out loud. I remember this: Tom and I in the shower together after that first night—steam rising like halos off our bodies, touching each other in places we'd discovered the night before as if those places had been transformed. Each touch, a confirmation of who we were now.

I was told my masseuse that day would be a masseur, an older man, blinded when he was seven by a Molotov cocktail. I have never had a massage by a man before, and I will admit to being a little tense, awaiting my masseur in the tiny room, naked on the table except for the light sheet covering my body. I open my eyes when, after a soft knock, he enters the room. He is older than me by many years. He wears a loose white shirt and trousers. The mottled skin of his face obvious even in the low light. A gray veil of blindness shades his eyes. He speaks English, though we hardly talk during the massage. I don't ask him about the Molotov cocktail and he doesn't ask me how long it's been since I've been touched. Neither does he ask why I am crying as, here on the massage table in this tiny, shadowed room in the intimate company of this blind man, a deep and familiar loneliness surfaces.

How does this feel to his hands, I wonder, as he reads my body with his touch? I want to ask him, "What does loneliness feel like? What is the texture of grief?"

His strong, wrinkled hands know their work well, and as he continues to find his way through the stories and secrets held by my body, it feels as if something essential and physical is released into the scented air, and my breath can find its way into places that, for months, have been covered over or covered up. I feel lighter.

After the massage, I shower, dress in my blue Greek coat, lavender Swedish mittens, and white Canadian mukluks, and go out into the cold, bright day to wait for Camille. How blue and clear the sky that afternoon, as if something essential and physical has been released from it, too. How light and beautiful the snow resting in the pink of still-blooming heather that lines the sidewalk.

Soon, Camille will return to America and I will go on my own again. But these last days of November, I just want to be. And to rest. Maybe you can't escape grief, I think; maybe you just have to learn to carry it. So, for now, it's safe to stay in Helsinki. Still, I know safe will wear on me, and with that feeling will come the urge to move to the next place. I know, for me, safe is not the answer.

CONFIDENCE CAPE

KELLY HUDSON

The familiar gnawing in the pit of my stomach woke me. I groaned and rolled over into a fetal position. My black cat, Sebastian, looked up at me, startled. "What? I'm hungry," I said and then grabbed him, scruffing up his head the way he liked. His purring filled the room.

I had run out of my food staples like spaghetti noodles and potatoes. A normal sixteen-year-old girl would have lived at home with her parents, but my parents had no home, so I was forced to share a townhome with three other housemates in their twenties. My sole piece of furniture? A mattress on the floor. My possessions? A few boxes of clothes and books in the corner. My curtains? A white sheet from Goodwill, with a large yellow sweat stain, tacked to the window.

Although I was working sixty hours a week, the first of the month was tight because all my money went to rent. I thought about eating at the Saint Francis Catholic Kitchen, shuffling my way through the assembly line with downcast eyes. I would need to pull my hair back into a braid to prevent catching lice. I imagined the look of pity from the person handing out plates. If I ran into someone from school volunteering to get social studies credit, I'd die from humiliation.

My head felt light, making it difficult to concentrate. I could feel the frustration growing inside me. *My parents should be able to help*. After all, I hadn't asked them for anything in months. I knew they received $400 of food stamps on the first of every month to take care of me. Since it was the fifth, I figured they would still have some left. I ran the numbers in my head. It would only take thirty dollars to tide me over until next payday, so I dressed quickly and took the bus downtown to locate them. Finding my homeless parents wasn't an easy task. When they were not in jail or the hospital, Mom and Dad hung out on the main drag of the Santa Cruz Pacific Garden Mall, selling crystals to tourists.

The first place I went was the alleyway near The Poet and Patriot Irish Pub. Fat Freddy, a bulky New Yorker with frizzy hair and a scruffy beard, was panhandling in the parking lot. When I was eight, Fat Freddy and Mom would drink a 40-ounce malt liquor for breakfast in this alley. Mom would break a food stamp, buy me a banana, then use the change to purchase a Mickey from the liquor store. "Your parents are at the other end of the mall," he said. I thanked him and walked down Pacific Avenue toward the clock tower.

It was midmorning and the cold air still clung to the fog that hadn't yet cleared. After about an hour, I finally found them underneath the red-and-black Pacific Cookie Company sign. I hadn't seen them in months, and they had each lost twenty pounds. They were skeletons of their former selves, like zombies in *Day of the Dead*.

Mom slouched against a planter box fifteen feet from Daddy, her brown hair parted in the middle and pulled into two neat braids. She looked out lazily in the distance with a flat smile and glassy eyes. She didn't see me. If she did, she would have straightened her posture and tried to compose herself. She would have hugged me with a suffocating fierceness and told me how much she missed me. Instead, she just stood there with her left arm hanging out. Her veins had all collapsed from needle usage. I shuddered and rubbed my left arm.

Daddy was sitting on the sidewalk. In front of him, on a gray wool army blanket, were a dozen clear quartz crystals and some necklaces. He was wrapping a crystal with silver wire to make a necklace and didn't see me approach. I took a deep breath. "Daddy?"

He looked up, dropped the necklace in his hands and jumped up to hug me. "Kelly girl!" He smelled like musty patchouli and vinegar. I backed away. The vinegar scent meant he was using again. His cheeks were splotchy and his arms were covered with a dozen open sores.

"I thought you went to rehab," I said, frowning.

"We're trying to get better." Daddy said, scratching his arm hard and fast like something crawled beneath his skin. "Don't give up on us." A scab popped off with a trickle of blood.

My heart was sinking, but I knew I had a job to do. *Thirty dollars to get me through the month.* I straightened my back and looked into his cloudy blue eyes. "Daddy … can I have some food stamps?" He frowned, pushing his graying hair behind his ears. He started coughing then turned and hacked up a loogie onto the curbside.

"I'm really hungry. All I need is thirty food stamps," I said.

Daddy's smile faded and he looked away. "Sorry, we don't have any right now."

My heart pounded fast. I backed away again and suddenly it all became clear. Instead of taking care of me, he was wasting the food stamps on heroin. My jaw clenched.

"That's bullshit," I said.

"I'm sorry, Kelly girl." Daddy shuffled his feet back and forth. "If you come find us in a couple weeks, I'll pull off a miracle." Instead of looking at me, he leaned down and picked up a crystal from the blanket, turning it over.

Suddenly, something inside me snapped. I couldn't afford to believe him anymore. I dug my fingernails deep into my palms until I felt the familiar sting.

Two weeks passed, but instead of going to see Daddy for that miracle, I went to the welfare office to kick them off food stamps. I wish I could say it was to prevent them from getting more drugs, but that's not true; I was pissed. *Why did I work my ass off while they got a handout?*

I got off the bus with indignant purpose, walking toward the two-story brick building. The waiting room was packed with forty people, mostly women who sat in the cheap brown bucket chairs, scowling at paperwork. A couple of kids laughed loudly as I entered, running past me like a pack of wild hyenas. Instead of cooling the lobby, the ceiling fans just pushed around the hot stuffy air.

My face flushed warm with defiance. I strolled up to the intake counter, grabbed the stack of paperwork and took a number, like Mom did countless times before. I turned, slowing as if moving through water. Every waiting room visit in a government office felt the same to me, as though time stood still.

Hours later, a heavyset woman sitting behind a thick plastic wall called my number. She grabbed the papers I pushed into her designated tray and started typing on the computer without looking at me. "What's the purpose for your visit?"

"I'm no longer living with my parents and want to cancel their food stamps." I suddenly felt confident in my black slacks, button-down collared shirt, and low-profile heels I had purchased on layaway at K-Mart. I felt it made me look sophisticated and grown up. I added, "I work full time and can take care of myself now."

She looked up from her computer for the first time, with apparent distaste. It might have been the same look she gave the cockroaches that scuttled out of her kitchen at night. *Does she think I'm worthless like my parents?*

"Good for you. Do you want a medal or something?" she said.

"What? No, I'm just saying that I don't need food stamps. But I need to stay on Medicaid because my jobs don't offer medical insurance."

"Do you have any kids?" she asked.

"No. I don't have kids. I'm sixteen."

She smacked her chewing gum and rolled her eyes. "Well honey, if you don't have kids, then you don't qualify for *any* public assistance. If you want to keep medical benefits, you can either go into foster care or you can get pregnant."

I stared at her in disbelief. She continued. "You currently get Medicaid because your parents receive benefits for you. But if you don't live with them, the only way to qualify on your own is to have kids. If you have a couple kids, you could get extra money for each one."

I tried to wrap my head around her words. Why would the government pay my medical costs while I was with my parents but not when I was on my own? Was she really telling me to get pregnant? A few of my best friends got pregnant in junior high, then dropped out of school and ended up on welfare. *I didn't want to end up like that.* I bit my lip, disgusted, and felt the metallic taste of blood. This clerk suddenly became the face of every person who assumed I would end up worthless like my parents.

From out of nowhere I yelled defiantly, "I will not get pregnant just to qualify for welfare! I'm going to find a better job that pays medical benefits, and when I'm old enough I'll vote against this social welfare bullshit."

I stormed out of the miserable office determined to prove I was worthy of more. Time slowed. A sense of lightness surrounded me, as if possibilities were making their way inside my head. In that moment of rejection, I realized that I had been blessed with freedom because I was no longer beholden to the system.

As I walked down the street, I imagined a shiny red confidence cape being placed on my shoulders. I straightened my back and walked tall, with renewed determination. Two months later, I went to court to officially become emancipated. Then I landed a job at a bank that paid enough money and offered great medical benefits.

Turns out I was my own miracle.

MOM, WE FOUND HER

SHAWNA RAWLINSON

"Mom, we found her."

"What, Shawnee?"

"We found her, I can't believe it, we found her," I said, crying and gasping for air. San Diegans had come out by the thousands to find Danielle, a seven-year-old, blond-haired, blue-eyed pretty little girl who had two brothers and played the piano. I led the team that recovered her remains—twenty-five days after she disappeared from her bed in the middle of the night. When a little girl went missing, I had to help; I just wasn't prepared to be the one to find her. Looking back, I can see the path that led me to her.

By the time I came along, both my parents were convicted felons. The night I was born, my father was incarcerated. He would remain there through my infancy and toddler years.

My mother, twenty-six, was a shrewd, successful drug dealer prone to violence. People didn't fuck with her. One of the first things Mom taught me was, "We don't talk to cops."

My sister, Mary Colette, was seven years older, a prodigy of criminal activity, manipulative and bold. She was my everything. I looked up to her, and she looked after and protected me. She could do anything with my fine, unmanageable hair: Bo Derek braids, Princess Leia buns.

"The good years," as I call them, were birth to age four, when my grandparents had us for most of the time. Then they died, along with everything that might have resembled normal.

The bad years started with Mom's manic moments. Morning bagpipes blared as we marched to the cemetery to picnic with dead grandparents. And then shopping for something we didn't need—like a raccoon or a pool table. Her lows would roll in like thunder, putting the house on lockdown, where you didn't dare make a noise.

Mom tried to pull it together by expanding her empire and moving up from smuggling marijuana in a Winnebago to manufacturing her own meth. Mom bought a beautiful house just above the ocean next to a golf course and left Dad behind. Colette ran track and was a popular girl. I took swimming lessons; we had horses at the stables. Things seemed quiet and normal for a minute, and quiet felt nice.

Then Mom went to prison for two years, just a slap on the wrist for stolen property, but the DA was after any conviction. I was six, and I saw her twice.

Mary Colette was thirteen and found a home with the SVLS, a Chicano street gang. They fed and clothed her and became her family. But being a gang member didn't protect her from rape—she never spoke her rapist's name.

I was placed in foster care with born-again Christians. They went to a creepy church where the parishioners spoke in tongues and fell to the ground. I'd seen stranger things than this; this was comedy. My foster uncle came over every weekend, and now I associate football with a man's hands in my pants.

I hate the Oakland Raiders.

Colette was fourteen when she met her pimp/boyfriend. He promised to give her the world and protect her from it at the same time. That was a great proposition to a girl on the streets. He gave her gifts and then took what was left of her innocence and her funds at the end of every shift.

Child human trafficking wasn't a term used in 1981; then they just called it pimpin' and ho-in'. And in the ghetto of east San Diego, it was the norm.

I was eight when Mom regained custody of me. I came home a little Jesus freak who was preoccupied with "saving" my family and drawing pictures of Jesus. Mom was the only one unchanged; still crazy, still ambitious, and ready to start dealing again. The rest of us were left to figure our own shit out.

Over the next four years, we followed our own paths amongst the craziness of our lives. I found safety in school, its structure a counterbalance to the chaos at home.

Colette had become a heroin addict and, at eighteen, a convicted prostitute with a rap sheet full of petty crimes. She was my sister, and I loved her deeply, but it hurt me to see her so sick with track marks up and down her frail, thin arms. Mom would rip her off the street and throw her into rehab, just to have her return every time. Then, one day, she disappeared; it was as if she had vanished into thin air. It was her birthday, her nineteenth birthday. October 23, 1985. One day, I had a sister that bullied and annoyed me. Then, in an instant, she was gone, and Colette was all I wanted.

Suddenly, Mom and I were on the same team, determined to bring Colette home and searching El Cajon Boulevard for any signs of her. We passed out missing posters and put them back up when they were torn down. One week dragged into a month, then into years. We searched all day and into the night—my mom and a car full of kids. Looking for our beautifully damaged Colette amongst the debris and discarded.

My mom had to fight the police just to get a missing person's report taken. Mary Colette Rawlinson entered the California Department of Justice database for missing persons in November of 1988—more than three years after her disappearance. She joined a list of forty-eight murdered young women. Without much evidence, the Homicide Task Force believed my sister was abducted and killed by one of three serial killers who ravaged El Cajon Boulevard from 1985 until 1988.

My mother had to change her policy on talking to cops.

I would spend my teens and twenties obsessed with Colette's disappearance, the other victims, and their killers. I would spend days at the library poring over what few articles were written about the lives that San Diegans would rather turn a blind eye to.

Fourteen. Fourteen articles were all I could find about the forty-nine victims. No one cared. Not the police, nor the media. All I could think about were the other women. Women like Colette who never made it to ink in the daily paper.

The first two years, our family was consumed with finding our Colette. And as Mom's depression grew, she gave up and vanished from our lives into her bedroom. Without her drug money, we were forced onto welfare—from the suburbs to a trailer park. Life was simply surviving. I was busy cashing welfare checks and trying to keep together what little family we had left. Tears would fall every night for my sister as my mind imagined what terrible things could have happened. Not knowing is the worst; sometimes my mind created scenarios too disturbing to accept as possible truths.

Never-ending questions were all our family had, but somehow I had this hope, this dream to find answers for another family. That's what drew me to search for Danielle.

"Mom, I need you. We found Danielle." I gasped, and a cry bellowed out from the center of my core. I fell to my knees, my head sunk in defeat, and I wept for that child as if she were my own.

"Shawna, catch your breath."

"Oh, my God, Mom, we found her."

"What?"

"We found Danielle." I sobbed.

"Baby, you brought that little girl home, something we will never have."

"But Mom, she's already haunting me. I can see what he did to her."

I know you want me to describe her. Everyone does. It's the question of all questions, and I get it all the time. I will judge you for it. It will change my perception of you forever. But you will ask—and I won't answer.

"This is what you wanted; this is the peace you asked for."

Peace? That will only come when we find Colette.

"Listen," she said softly, "you're strong, Shawna, stronger than you know."

"I love you, Mom." I'd always had to be her anchor, but now I knew Mom could be mine too.

I became the story within the story. Sister of missing girl finds missing girl. The next day, I graced the front page of the *San Diego Union-Tribune*, and the title read,

Successful Searchers Guided by Angel

And next to my name was my sister's. It read, "Mary Colette Rawlinson, missing fourteen years, and feared dead." Someone finally saw it fit to give Colette what she deserved all along. For her town, the city she was born in, to give a fuck enough to report that she was missing. And it didn't stop there. The next day the *New York Times* picked up the story, as did thousands of papers around the country.

The day after that, the media emerged like vultures at my mother's front door, searching out the anomaly of a searcher guided by her angel sister. My mother would beam with pride as she offered coffee to the reporters clamoring to obtain the gruesome details. Meanwhile, I hid in silence, dealing with my new torment, the terrors through the night, and the constant images of a dead little girl—that would be my payment for a job well done.

The sacred rules of community don't apply to everyone; I learned that thirty-two years ago, to this very day. Everything gets its own priority. A seven-year-old girl, of a well-to-do family, has been found. A drug-addicted prostitute can wait.

THE MAASAI IN THE MIRROR

ELIZABETH OPPEN ESHOO

The tallest of the Maasai warriors walked over to me and stood inches from my face, spear in one hand, shield in the other, somewhere in the middle of the East African bush. He was so close to me, in fact, that I could hear the buzz from the swarm of flies feasting on the whites of his eyes and could smell the smoky residue of burned cow dung infused in the bright-red cloth he wore so elegantly draped over his right shoulder.

Nothing in my Waspy upbringing had prepared me for this moment, other than knowing to be absolutely polite and respectful to my host … who just so happened to be *a Maasai warrior.*

Despite the primal fear I felt in his presence, something in the innermost depth of my being knew I was born to be standing precisely there in that moment, as though my whole life had led me to this place, to this young man who was venturing out into the world on his own journey. As a warrior in training, he was living in the bush away from the safety of his family, learning what it meant to be of service to his fellow Maasai, to be brave in the face of a lion, and *to become a man.*

I too was venturing forth in the world to begin my *own* journey, in hopes of discovering how to become a different kind of warrior. To be brave and face my own fears, to figure out who I wanted to be in the world. I had always been an achiever type, more concerned with racking up accolades than pursuing what fulfilled me on the inside.

Until I got a wake-up call from my doctor, informing me that my insides had turned cancerous. As if that weren't enough, my heart broke when I found out my boyfriend had been cheating on me our entire two-year relationship. It shattered again when I learned my friends had known all along.

At age twenty-six, I stepped off the conveyor belt of my New York City corporate life and realized I had not been living an authentic life. I'd been so good at following all the rules and pleasing all the grown-ups, that I lost track of who I was. Despite my success, I felt like an imposter, acting out a narrative that didn't fit my own true story. I came to Africa broken.

Facing the fear of my mortality, I did what any habitual overachiever would do—I signed up for an Outward Bound course. My plan was to climb Mt. Kilimanjaro in hopes of figuring it all out. I traded in my Ann Taylor suits and my Coach briefcase for a pair of leather hiking boots and a backpack to begin my African journey of self-discovery.

There was a secret language to living in this part of the world and just four days into my adventure, I hadn't yet learned to speak it. Being here in this strange place fast-tracked life lessons, grabbed me by the collar, shook me out of my sleepy state, and demanded I finally pay attention. With all the comforts and crutches of home stripped away, I had to discover who I was in this place. *Who was I, period?*

I'd been resting in my tent when I felt the thunderous arrival of what I imagined was a herd of wildebeests. I poked my head out and saw, instead, thirty or so intimidating Maasai warriors, all dressed sparingly in bits of red cloth, carrying shields and spears and hand-carved wooden clubs in their muscled arms. I feared we had pissed them off, intruded upon their land perhaps, and that we needed to pack up and leave.

That's when I noticed the tallest of all the warriors. He was away from the others, standing at the washbasin table outside my tent. He held up two round shaving mirrors; one pointed at the front of his face and one at the back of his head, admiring his neatly plaited hair. He was moving the position of the mirrors this way and that. I wondered if he'd ever seen his face before, or the back of his head. *Was this the first time he'd seen the whole of himself?*

I exited the tent to see what this was all about, when suddenly the group of warriors formed a half circle around the firepit and began jumping up and down in place, easily clearing a good three feet of space with every jump. They looked like marionettes being pulled to the sky by an invisible string.

Surrounded by these regal and beautiful indigenous beings, I felt a shift, a sense of wildness well up from deep within me. *Like I too could jump three feet off the ground with no effort.* Their tall, muscled bodies, the elegant way they stood, the absolute confidence emanating from them, filled me with awe and reverence and made me feel that much more a stranger here. I'd never met other human beings with such pure authenticity.

As fascinated as we were by these young men, they likewise were fascinated by us. We stood before them: white; short, medium and tall; young and old; clad in hiking boots, colorful shorts, and an array of sunglasses and hats. Without a common language between us, we used our bodies and eyes to communicate.

That's when the tall one walked right up to me and reached out his sinewy arm and touched my long brown hair. I held my breath as I stood before him, *still as prey in the crosshairs of a poacher's rifle.* He ran his fingers through my strands as he held his spear in one hand, my hair in the other.

His power-filled hands, the ones that gripped his spear, that had made his buffalo-skin shield, that hunted the mighty lion—unimaginable tasks for this city girl who used her soft, manicured hands to hail taxi cabs along Park Avenue—his hands transmitted a kindness, a curiosity, a gentleness I never would have imagined. I felt seen by him—treasured, validated, admired—all with one touch.

What about *me* drew the attention of this towering warrior? Why did he reach for my plain brown hair instead of the long blond manes or curly locks of the other girls? Did this Maasai warrior have a special power to see beyond the color of my hair or the arrangement of my face, to look inside me and read my soul like he read danger upon the African plains? *What did he see in me that I could not?*

His simple gesture transmitted volumes to me. I wondered—how could I communicate with him? If only I could speak his language or if he could speak mine! The social rules of my conventional upbringing did not apply here.

So in the stillness of the bush, I shed my reticence and dared to reach out to him, to make a connection the only way I could think of: to touch the cluster of colorful beads he had woven so artfully into the array of little braids on his head.

We paused like that for a moment; for a split second, we were connected. In the stillness, when our hands reached out to each other, I think he transferred some of his wildness to me. I felt my being crack open—bright light, fresh air, a freedom unveiled in just a single moment with just a single touch. It had been there all along, but buried, hidden—*even from me.*

No words between us, just a human-to-human connection that in its starkness allowed me to see who I was. As though I too were holding up two mirrors for the first time and was able to see myself fully. Standing toe-to-toe with the Maasai warrior, I saw my reflection in him and realized: I am enough, just as I am.

I too am a warrior.

THE LIFT

CHERIE KEPHART

A black Chevrolet approached. Squinting from the sun bouncing off the glistening metal, I attempted to make eye contact with the driver, but the sun shone too bright. With my right leg stiff in a brace, I hobbled toward the car and found my way into the back seat. The driver glanced at me through the rearview mirror. His gray hair matched the car's dull interior. The skin around his eyes drooped and the faint smell of gas station coffee lingered around him.

He scanned his phone. "Says here you're going to Sorrento Valley, that right?"

I hadn't spoken to anyone yet that day. I cleared my throat. "Yes, thanks."

I clicked the seat belt in place and settled in for the forty-five-minute drive. The piercing pain in my leg had kept me up most of the night. Warm and secure in the car, my eyelids closed, and I didn't fight it.

The car barreled down the road at a quick but smooth clip as talk radio murmured through the speakers. A few minutes later, the driver's baritone voice startled me out of my light doze. "You watch the third presidential debate last night?"

I opened my eyes and at the same time I heard the names Donald Trump and Hillary Clinton. Political talk radio. Was I still dozing? Donald J. Trump, the man known for money, for gold hotels and towers laced with bankruptcy and shady deals, for firing people on reality TV, and for a crazy, Creamsicle-colored comb-over, was running for president of our United States?

He was. I knew it. I had been paying attention. I hoped it wasn't real, but it was.

I didn't like discussing politics, especially recently. The polarization between the Democrats and the Republicans was palpable. I swallowed hard. "Yes, I did."

We were stopped at a traffic light. The driver turned the dial down on the radio, peered over his shoulder and asked, "So, what'd you think?"

Oh no. Not that question. Anything but that.

What did I think? I didn't like it. Either side, really. The debate was more like junior-high-schoolers running for class president, complete with adolescent name-calling. *What was becoming of our country?* I took a slow breath in, choosing my words with caution. "I wasn't fond of either candidate's presentation of the issues or the way they handled them."

The driver picked up a pair of aviator sunglasses that were chipped all around the edges and secured them on his face. As the light turned green, he stepped on the gas and the touchy throttle propelled us past two other cars up the hill on the way to the freeway entrance. He tightened his grip on the steering wheel. "Well, I think Hillary's a liar and Trump's the guy to put this country back on track. We need someone to get things done, no matter what the cost."

I felt a slight twinge in my stomach. My life was in this guy's hands, so I certainly didn't want to debate politics. I wanted to choose silence, but my face turned flush and I instinctively clenched my jaw. My silence lasted all of five seconds.

"What do you mean, no matter what the cost?"

He shrugged. "Look, I wasn't all in for Trump in the beginning, but I definitely don't want Hillary for president. All the stuff she's done. No thank you. Besides, Trump won't let anyone stand in his way. He's willing to do whatever it takes."

The driver twisted the wheel and with a sharp motion the vehicle accelerated onto the freeway, zero to seventy-five in only a few seconds. I wanted to get out of the car, to ask him to pull over. But it was too late. The next words flew out of my mouth with force. "You're right. Trump is willing to do whatever it takes. Have you thought about how he accomplishes this? By stepping on people. Is that the kind of president we want?"

The driver's voice escalated. "Absolutely. Sometimes we need to step on people to get things done."

Whoa. I clenched my fists and accidently bit my tongue. I tasted blood. "I'm sorry, but where I come from, it's *never* okay to step on people."

The veins in his neck throbbed and he jutted his chin out. My response must have triggered something deep in him, for he embarked on a political monologue featuring all the things he liked about Trump and loathed about Hillary. "Trump doesn't care what people think," he shouted, "so it frees him to get things accomplished."

My heart rate quickened and dizziness overcame me. I took a deep breath and glanced out the window, noticing the Torrey pines lining the hill near the beach. I tried to wish my vertigo away, but it plagued me, just like the painful cyst behind my knee that kept me from driving. As I watched the beach scenery slide by, I massaged my temples. The driver finally stopped talking.

After a few moments, he let out a series of curt, rapid groans. I glanced at him, he was rubbing his neck.

I lifted my head and took in a deep, calming breath. *I could change this.*

"So, do you do this driving thing full-time?" I asked.

He tilted his head and peered beneath his sunglasses. "Now I do, yeah."

"What'd you do before this?"

"I was a commercial airline pilot for about thirty years."

"Why'd you stop?"

"My eyesight was starting to go. You can't fly if you can't see."

What? I felt a little acid rise in my throat as we barreled down the freeway now doing almost eighty.

"Don't worry. I can see fine for driving, just not up to snuff by aviation standards."

My shoulders relaxed. I felt the energy between us shift. "Where'd you learn how to fly?"

"I was a pilot in Vietnam. Learned most of what I know from that."

I felt my heart, which had moments ago been encased in anger, soften. He was a veteran. I was a veteran too. A veteran of more than twenty years of health challenges since serving in the United States Peace Corps in Africa. I wanted to help people, to serve my country through peace, by giving back. In return, I've spent years in pain, trying not to die. But I would never compare myself to a veteran of war. The turmoil and torture of war was something I would never understand.

"Thank you for putting your life on the line for all of us. That must've been tough."

He placed his sunglasses on his head and gave me a subtle nod. "I could write a book about everything I've been through."

"I'm certain you could." Then I chuckled. "I just finished writing a memoir about almost dying from a chronic, undiagnosed illness. The book's coming out soon."

The car came to a slow halt as we exited the freeway and approached a red traffic light. The rearview mirror revealed tears leaking out the corners of his eyes.

"My daughter's been sick seven years. Doctors can't figure out what's wrong with her."

The softness around my heart grew even bigger. I knew his daughter's pain. It was my pain.

He sniffed. "Sorry to hear all you've had to go through. Must be awful."

His compassion poured through me like a wave of light.

For the rest of the ride, we shared stories about my illness and his daughter's condition. What we both had tried. How people thought we were crazy. We even spoke of the unspeakable. The times I wanted to end it all. The times he saw his daughter right there too.

We finally arrived at my doctor's office. The driver turned toward me, and I reached out my hand. He shook it and smiled.

I flashed a smile back. "Thank you for the lift. Tell your daughter she's not alone."

He released my hand and gave a solid nod. I exited the car and began to limp toward the clinic, turning to watch the Chevrolet barrel back onto the street—on to the next passenger.

I suddenly realized I never even got his name. But it didn't matter. I knew him. He was just like me.

SECRET SON

LAURA L. ENGEL

I remember brilliant stars sprinkling in a cloudless sky. Cool, crisp October air. I was out walking my dogs before heading to bed, planning a peaceful night of reading, when my iPhone pinged. Glancing down, I stopped in my tracks. It was an email from Ancestry.com.

The message read,

> *Parent/Child Match.*

I stared at the screen, eyes and mouth wide open. I nearly fell to my knees. My throat closed and my heart pounded erratically. Fight-or-flight adrenaline kicked in. Forgetting the dogs, I ran back into the house, passing my stunned husband, Gene.

"What is it? What happened?" he called out.

I could not answer as I dropped in the chair in front of my desktop computer, my fingers frantically hitting the wrong keys as I logged onto Ancestry.com.

The email was straightforward, businesslike:

> *I just received my DNA profile from Ancestry.com. It says we are a parent/child match. I was adopted, and I am looking for more information. – Richard R. Ray*

Tears streamed down my face. Terrified yet thrilled, my thoughts turned to the tiny flat wooden box that had traveled with me across the country, moving place to place, holding my deepest secret, a symbol of the loss that changed the direction of my life, colored my days, and, at times, crushed my spirit. The box contains one item: a small, frayed birth card, creased where I had folded it and stuffed it in my pocket 49 years ago. It was the only tangible proof of the baby boy I had given birth to in the summer of 1967.

On this fall evening in 2016, my body trembling, my heart in my throat, I found myself again a seventeen-year-old girl, dropped off at an unwed mothers home in New Orleans, alone and scared. Without support from my family or the father of my child, a teenage boy himself, I was made to feel like damaged goods or a criminal.

There were no organizations, education, or assistance for young women in my condition. No alternatives, I was assured. In the end, I had been forced to relinquish my firstborn son for adoption, a baby boy I named Jamie.

Society in the sixties did not treat unwed mothers kindly. I was told I would never see him again. Everyone said, "Never speak of this. Forget him. It's for the best."

Forgetting had been impossible. I had carried that child for nine months. He would always be part of me, and I had thought about him every day of every year. Now, sitting at the computer, I stared at the screen.

Could this be happening? My God, could this be the beautiful baby I held and cried over as he was taken from me? My Jamie? My son? All these years of wondering what he looked like. Where he lived.

If he was happy. Healthy. Who else could it be? It had to be him. Richard. Richard? God help me. Please let it be him.

Gene hurried into our home office after rescuing our baffled pups. "Laura! What is it?"

"Oh, honey, listen to this," I cried. With difficulty, I read the email aloud.

Tears sprang to his eyes as he hugged me close, saying "I knew this would happen one day, Laura. Do you think it's really him?"

"I don't know. But no, yes, oh God … Yes, I do know. I know it's him."

Who is this man? Will he hate me for giving him up? Can he forgive me? Can I explain what happened?

For years, I had longed for this day, secretly praying I would find him. I had researched how to find him, entered my name and data on countless search websites, and finally had submitted my DNA to Ancestry.com. Now he had found me—through DNA—on the internet! This was something I could never have dreamed possible in 1967.

So why, dear God, was I so afraid? How strange to have wanted this for all those long years and to now feel paralyzed with fear. I had pushed this secret so far down, and now it was bubbling up, scaring me in a whole new way. I realized I'd never thought past finding Jamie. *If this was my son, my Jamie, why was I not jumping for joy? Why this fear?*

Painful, buried memories bubbled to the surface. Only a handful of people in my life had even known about his birth. Mama and Daddy had refused to acknowledge it had happened, and they had died decades later, never mentioning that time in our lives.

Their lives were over. How will this affect our lives? My family? His family? Richard? They named him Richard?

"What are you going to do?" Gene asked.

"I don't know. I don't want to scare him away. What if he doesn't write back? What if he hates me? What if he thinks I didn't want him?"

"He won't hate you." As always, Gene was the voice of reason.

I wrote back:

> *My heart is doing flip-flops, but can you please tell me the date of your birth and the place you were born?*

I sat back and exhaled. *It might take awhile before he answers*, I assured myself.

The wait was only a few seconds. I jumped as the answer popped up on the screen.

> *July 8, 1967. New Orleans, Louisiana.*

My heart stopped. "It's him! It's him! It has to be. It's Jamie!"

July 8, 1967, had been imprinted on my heart. I knew without a doubt and with all my soul—this was my son, Jamie, who signed his name "Richard." My hands trembled so badly I could barely type, but type I did. Nonstop, for hours.

For hours, we emailed, asking questions, cautiously sidestepping around each other, trying to come to terms with the miracle taking place. Our emails changed from one or two hesitant sentences to lengthy missives in which we poured out our hearts to each other. In just a couple of hours, I knew more about Richard than I ever dreamed I would. It was exhausting. It was beautiful.

I learned that Richard had been raised in Alexandria, Louisiana, that he'd had a happy life with loving adoptive parents. He wrote,

> *I have had a good life. I have always known I was adopted from as far back as I remember.*

He had been adopted at five weeks of age. Now a husband and father of three children, he was an assistant attorney general for the state of Louisiana. He had lived a secure and fortunate life.

My mind on overload, I answered his questions—about me, the family he had never known existed.

> *I live in California. You have three half-brothers. A day did not pass that I did not think or wonder about you.*

As amazed as I was at that moment, the overwhelming guilt and sorrow I had felt for forty-nine years tore at my soul. My conscience screamed, "You should have been raising this son with your other sons!" I was simultaneously happy for him and jealous of his adoptive parents, yet grateful for them. Intellectually, I knew I had not been given a choice.

But, could I have fought more to keep him?

I was stunned when I opened a text and saw a photo of Richard smiling on the screen. He looked like he had sprung from me alone. I studied those photos of him and his children with awe and longing. DNA shouted from the screen. This is my son! Thrilled, yet heartbroken to have missed his life, I sobbed afresh.

This man is my son. This is my Jamie.

A message from Jamie appeared.

> *I will call you tonight, at 7 p.m. your time. Is that ok?*

I typed,

> *Of course, of course!*

My thoughts whirled: *How could I wait three more hours to speak to him? What would my parents have thought if they were still alive? This man was their first grandson. Here was the baby boy who they had not allowed me to keep, all grown up. Would they have been happy for me? What will my sons say? What will anyone say?*

My dark, painful secret was out: *How will I explain this secret son?*

Immediately, my thinking shifted from years of shame and worry to "I don't give a damn what anyone says or thinks." All the years of holding this pain inside of myself melted away. I longed to shout to the world, "My son has found me! This is a miracle!"

When the phone rang precisely at 7 p.m., I grabbed it and squeaked, "Hello, is it you?"

"Yes, it's me." I instinctively knew this soft, masculine southern voice. My heart soared. "I know your voice," he said in awe.

We laughed and cried as I began telling him the story of his beginnings and my life. And he told me the story of his. After I hung up four hours later, I reran that conversation in my mind, again and again. How can I describe my feelings? They defy words. Still, I will try.

I can only describe it as similar (yet not the same) as the delirious happiness a new mother feels after she gives birth and kisses the velvety head of her newborn, ecstatically counting his tiny fingers and toes. The amazing bliss of looking at that perfect and wondrous miniature human being and proudly thinking, *I did this. This precious child is part of me*. It was that crazy, insane joy you feel when you first bring your new infant home.

It was all of that, yet more. It was richly layered because, while tinged with a loss I could not deny, I had seen that baby's future. I knew that he was loved in his childhood by adoring parents. That he was given a remarkable life. That he was now an adult, a kind man, a decent human being, a father who loves his children, a husband who loves his wife, a man devoted to and beloved by his family and friends.

A man determined to find and know his birth mother. A smile like no other graced my face. We had found each other. My son, my son.

CAT SCAN

BARBARA HUNTINGTON

"Are you about ready to leave for the hospital?"

I had decided to call before heading out the door to meet my niece and my mom at the hospital for Mom's CAT scan and wanted to be sure they would arrive on time.

"No, Grandma has decided she doesn't want to go."

"What? Oh, no. Let me talk with her." I held the phone with one hand as my other pressed cold fingers against my hot, churning stomach.

Dr. Fisher, my husband's Parkinson's neurologist, had set up the appointment after agreeing to evaluate Mom for Alzheimer's, and I had finally gotten it all together. What the hell was going on?

"Hey, Mom, I am looking forward to seeing you at the hospital for your CAT scan in a little while; are you coming?"

"Of course, honey." Her voice was strong, considering her recent hip replacement and loss of my stepfather, who had stayed with her day and night in the hospital, picked up the H1N1 virus, and died twenty days later.

After reaffirming this change of heart with my niece, my little blue Civic and I had headed up the 805 and I was now pacing the waiting room—no Mom. Soon the screen on my cell phone announced my niece.

"We're on the freeway, but we talked to Aunt Helen and she says Grandma doesn't have to get a CAT scan if she doesn't want to and Grandma is screaming she wants me to turn the car around."

"Let me talk to her."

"Mom, I am at the hospital waiting to see you. Will you be here soon?" (I didn't mention her sister Helen's comments.)

"Yes, honey. I look forward to seeing you, too."

Although she had heard the whole conversation, when she got back on the line, my niece said she was not happy but was driving on. Having heard my end of the conversation, the nurse at the desk agreed to have a wheelchair at the door when they arrived.

As soon as Mom's purplish-pink SUV arrived, driven by my niece, I opened the passenger door. Mom was on the cell phone with my brother. Grabbing the phone, I said something inane like, "I've gotta get her inside," and hung up.

Easing Mom into the chair, I then wheeled her in, with my niece yelling that she didn't have to have a CAT scan. The cell phone Mom had been holding rang, and I answered it to hear my brother screaming at me about my having no right to hang up on him, so I hung up again. A nurse grabbed the chair, hustling us up a waiting elevator to the second floor.

After Mom and I chattered softly for a long time, I flagged down a nurse who told us, "Those people she came in with were threatening to call the police, but we had the orders and you have power of attorney, so we are going ahead."

Mom raised no resistance and smiled as she entered the machine. After the scan, I held her hand as Mom whispered, "I love it when you fight over me."

SITTING IN

NATALIE FREEDMAN

At 8 a.m., I walked into Walgreens with the other board members of our volunteer group, PACE, Public Accommodations for Everyone. Larry, Preston, and Decker were young black men. Eugene, Brad, and I were white.

My stomach was churning with fear and my mouth felt dry. The smells of bacon and coffee hung in the air. At intervals on the counter there were round plastic containers filled with slices of pies and cakes. The counter was green Formica and I counted eighteen stools, all filled with customers, many of whom turned when we entered. Did they know what we were planning? Maybe a sit-in in Phoenix was not a good idea.

Eugene put a reassuring hand on my shoulder. "Just remember everything we practiced yesterday."

"The problem is we might not have thought of everything that could happen," said Decker. "And I certainly don't relish the idea of going to jail like those college kids last month in Baltimore."

"At least Larry and Brad and I are lawyers," said Eugene.

"You may be lawyers and familiar with court and all, but Preston and I have to face our father. And he's madder than hell, says it will reflect badly on the mortuary. He says it will be bad for business."

Brad was at the counter, eating an omelet. When he saw us, he stood up. "Natalie, take my seat." A pleasant young waitress, her hair all covered by a net, took my order. I ordered one scrambled egg with toast. But the plan was not to eat it, so I'd eaten at home. My stomach was fluttering so badly that I probably couldn't have eaten it anyway.

Eugene, Brad, Decker, and Larry stood behind me with about six other people, waiting for seats. A motherly black woman came over to the counter and patted Larry's arm. "You get served in the COLORED TO GO line," she said to him. "You can get coffee and some baked goods. They don't make you any hot food, but you can get you a hard-boiled egg. And then you gots to take your food out the door. You can eat at the bus bench. That's how it's run."

"I know how it's run," said Larry. "But I went to law school so I could run it differently."

Eugene had told us all to dress professionally. The four men—three lawyers and one mortician—were all in fine suits with white shirts and subdued ties. I was wearing a conservative plum-colored dress with low black heels. I had pearls around my neck and pearl earrings.

An older man dressed in overalls in the COLORED TO GO line spoke to Larry. "Listen, boy, don't make any trouble for us now." He was scared, his forehead wrinkled.

The lady sitting next to me now got up with her little boy. Decker and Larry sat down in the two empty seats. The entire counter stared at them. A man eating a bagel shouted out, "Hey, you guys can't sit there. Go to the COLORED TO GO line."

My waitress, in her yellow uniform with her name tag, ELLEN, slid my plate of eggs and toast down and stared at the two black men next to me.

"I'll just have oatmeal and whole wheat toast and coffee," said Decker casually.

"You know you're not allowed at the counter. You get your food over there and go. I can't serve you nothing."

"I'll have the $5.99 special, with ham, not sausage," said Larry in his cultured New York accent.

Ellen's eyes darted around. Without another word, she walked to the kitchen and an older woman, her gray hair also in a net, came out wiping her hands. Her nametag read, CONNIE.

"We're not allowed to serve you men here. It's against the rules of Walgreens and we have to follow their rules." She turned to me. "Ma'am, you haven't touched your food. If you don't want it, could you please give up your seat to them that's waiting?" Ten people were waiting.

"I'm going to just sit here until you serve my friends," I said.

"You can't take up the seat, lady. We're not serving them and you'd be here all day."

A pleasant-looking grandmotherly woman behind me said, "Yes, young lady, you're being very rude. I need to sit down; my legs are killing me."

Another woman in a lovely tan suit walked up behind me. "I have to get to my office! Get up!"

When I said nothing, she leaned over and hissed, "Nigger lover!" And here it was not even 9 a.m. yet. I kept my eyes in front of me. Eugene, behind me, stepped closer. Ellen and Connie went back into the kitchen and out came an older man, his hair also in a net.

"Look, I'm the cook here. We don't want no trouble. But we're not serving you and you're taking up two seats during our morning rush."

"Why can't you serve us?" asked Decker.

"Because you're black," said the cook.

Decker took out his wallet and waved several $10 bills. "Our money is green. We're sitting here courteously, not bothering anybody. He's a lawyer and I'm a businessman. And we want to eat breakfast."

"We're not going to serve you. Our store manager comes in at ten and he'll take some action. Probably call the cops on you."

There was muttering behind us. Two white men in telephone company uniforms said, "Do you want us to drag them out? We could take them on."

"These men are our colleagues," said the six-foot-four, solidly built Eugene. The telephone company men looked Eugene up and down and sat down at the end of the counter as a couple got up.

The middle-aged woman sitting next to me said, "Don't you have something better to do than causing a fuss? I see you have a wedding ring. Are you married to one of those Negroes?"

I thought, no, I'm married to Philip, a man I love desperately, who has argued with me all week about participating in this sit-in. "I don't want you to get hurt. Anything could happen. You have a one-year-old child. I know you want to stop discrimination, but this stunt is too dangerous." Finally, exasperated, he'd said, "I can't stop you, I suppose. I agree with your cause, you know I do, but I don't want my wife doing it."

And it was worse with my scrutinizing mother-in-law, visiting us from Los Angeles. "This is one of the stupidest things you've ever done, Natalie. You want to change the natural order of things. You know you're only making colored people more uppity. I told you when you were registering colored people to vote that no good would come of it. Those colored people won't be content with just voting. They're going to want to run things; they're going to want to be all over the place. You're a Jewish girl. This isn't even your fight."

"It's 1960," I'd said. "It's every American's fight."

The two women standing behind me seemed to echo my mother-in-law's thoughts. "Be reasonable, dear," one of them said to me. "You're not going to change anything." The other woman hit me in the back with her heavy purse, and it was not an accident.

Behind us, in a low voice, Eugene said, "Calm. Nonviolent. Mahatma Gandhi," reminding us of the training we'd had. It was now nine thirty, and Eugene and Brad found seats at the counter.

"We'll order when you serve our friends," said Brad.

So we sat there. About an hour later, a man in a rumpled suit came up to us. "I'm the store manager," he said. His badge read, MR. TURLEY. "You can't just sit there. See our sign? We reserve the right to refuse service to anyone. If you're not out of those chairs by eleven thirty, I'm calling the police. We get a good crowd here for lunch."

"Bring the five of us our orders and we'll eat and go," said Eugene.

The lunch crowd seemed even angrier than the breakfast people. "This is outrageous!" said one woman. "I only get forty minutes to eat," said one man. All of a sudden, I felt a little thud in my head. Someone had spit into my hair. I wiped it away with a napkin, shuddering.

Two uniformed policemen arrived and Mr. Turley pointed out who we were. "Arrest all five of them," said Mr. Turley.

One of the policemen leaned in to talk to Decker and Larry. "Look, you've made your point. Get up now and go about your business before there's any trouble."

"We're not causing any trouble, Officer. Just waiting for our food," said Larry.

Eugene gave each of the policemen a PACE card. "It's a nonprofit organization to provide equality for all in restaurants and hotels. We want to end discrimination in Phoenix."

"Have they broken anything, taken anything?" the policemen asked Mr. Turley. "We can't arrest them unless they've done something illegal."

"They're taking up our seats," said Mr. Turley. "If that's not illegal, it should be."

"We have another call, so we have to leave," said one policeman, and they left.

Now in came a man carrying a camera and a sign that read NBC NEWS. A blond woman, heavily made up, interviewed us. "We're on the board of PACE," said Eugene. "We feel that all people should be able to eat where they wish as long as they can afford it."

"Could you tell our TV audience why you're doing this?" she asked me.

The lights were hot on my face but I looked directly into the camera. "I have a little daughter and I want my child to grow up in a city where people can be served regardless of their color."

"They've been here for seven hours," said Mr. Turley. He turned to us in rage. "Now, you've brought the TV in on us. I'm calling our corporate office in Chicago."

At four o'clock, I was tired and had to go to the bathroom, and the building crowd waiting behind us was growing exasperated. A seat was vacated and Preston, Decker's brother, swiftly sat down.

"Another black man," said a man behind us. "He thinks because he's dressed up in a suit, he can eat with us."

At almost five, Mr. Turley was back. There were about eight people waiting for stools behind us. "Serve them," said Mr. Turley to Ellen. "From that old pot."

Sullenly, lips pressed together, Ellen gave all six of us each a lukewarm cup of coffee, and Decker put down a $20 bill. We took one sip of the awful coffee and thanked them.

"Will I be served at Walgreens tomorrow?" asked Larry.

"Corporate says so. Not at all their lunch counters. Just Arizona and Illinois."

"What is this country coming to?" wailed an older lady. "We have to eat with colored people now." A mixed sensation of exhaustion and jubilation crept up as we exchanged victorious glances.

Before we walked out, we took long sips of the coffee. It was cold, thick, grainy, and tasteless. It was the best cup of coffee I ever had.

TRADING POST

DONNA JOSE

It was the flyer next to the cash register that caught my attention. It said, "Don't Miss It! Tonight at the Lakeside Trading Post – a psychic reading circle with Medium Betty Silva."

So I'm scanning the details, including the ninety-dollar cost, when a female voice says, "She's gifted. You should come." The voice, I learn, belongs to Elizabeth, the Trading Post's owner, and the organizer of the event.

I told her ninety dollars seemed a little steep for a group reading.

"You won't be disappointed," she says. "She's that good. Clearest medium I've ever come across."

Now, even though Elizabeth obviously has an interest in promoting Betty and her event, she has set me wondering. Wondering is bad. Wondering costs me money when satisfaction is only fifty-fifty. It's not that I haven't paid as much or more for a "good" reading, but even then I've thought the price too high. Yet there's no bargaining over cost with the typical psychic, as prices are set by supply and demand—even in the occult world. All I can do is take my business elsewhere.

But, it's too late. I'm intrigued. Just how good is this Betty? What would I miss by walking away? Was it fate that brought me here? I try to turn the volume down in my brain, but I am vulnerable.

"Sign me up," I tell Elizabeth. "My daughter and I will be back at seven for the circle." We haggle for the next five minutes over whether my thirteen-year-old daughter, Taliesin, may attend as an observer without paying. I prevail.

When we return, the Trading Post has been transformed. Candlelight bounces around the space, illuminating the faces of my fellow seekers. We are a diverse group. There's a buttoned-up businesswoman on my daughter's left, and I'm guessing the Harley parked out front belongs to the biker-type seated on my right.

"You're skeptical," Betty says to the biker. He nods his head up and down. Tattoos and piercings decorate his body. There are rings on each of his fingers. Colored bandanas wind round his neck.

"Your brother in spirit is here. You are like brothers. Yes?"

"Yes," he responds.

"I use the present tense because this bond cannot be broken by death. Do you understand this?"

"Yes," he says.

"Your brother is saying it was a bike accident. Head trauma. He lingered for days." She pauses and cocks her head to one side. "There was nothing that could be done. Nothing you could have done. He wants you to know this."

The biker sits expressionless as Betty continues.

"You blame yourself."

This time he nods a "yes," but it is almost imperceptible. Then Betty does something that I have never seen in a psychic circle before. She asks him if she can approach him.

When he agrees, Betty takes several steps toward him, and as she does, he stands and strides toward her. She extends her right hand to shake his. He thrusts his hand forward to meet hers. *We* think she proposes a simple handshake, but this isn't her intention at all. At once *he* realizes what's happening and joins her in what becomes a fluid dance between the two of them.

A secret handshake? A biker handshake? This is unbelievable, but when it's done and the "brother" returns to his seat, I can tell even in the dim light that his eyes are brimming with tears. I can feel the emotion he's trying so hard to contain. He sits stoically, ramrod straight, his hands gripping the arms of his chair, looking straight ahead, not saying a word to the woman who has brought him here.

Of course, this could all be staged, I think. It is so beyond anything I have ever experienced, but as Betty addresses one person and then another, we witness revelations and healings all around. Surely, my daughter and I aren't the only "real" customers.

I'm holding Taliesin's hand in my lap when Betty calls my name. Taliesin withdraws as Betty takes a few moments to orient herself to me. Her eyes are closed, and the tops of her fingertips brush her lips as if she's in prayer. Then, she opens her eyes, drops her hands to her sides, and addresses me.

"There's a woman here who .... "

I cut her off mid-sentence. "I only want to hear from my husband." I say.

Of course, now I've given her key information about myself, but after what I've seen here tonight it probably doesn't matter. Betty brings her fingertips back to her lips and closes her eyes again. After about twenty seconds, she speaks.

"So that you know I have your husband now, I'm going to make a sound that he says you will recognize." And then she inhales and makes the unmistakable sound of taking a drag on a doobie.

I am shocked. The biker laughs out loud. But Betty has just proved herself. I'm now a believer, because no one knows that my husband still indulged at his age except the guy he bought the pot from and me.

"You've got him," I say. (I want to move things along before my young daughter starts asking questions!)

Betty continues. "This was recent. He says it was his heart. Very fast. Very unexpected." She brings her hand to her chest. "He says he came back for a moment. Does this make sense to you?"

This one I have to think about, but then it falls into place. As he lay lifeless on the living room floor, I knelt down between his legs and began rubbing them up and down, calling him back to life with my voice. I didn't know what else to do. The heart monitor that was right there was flat.

When I started touching him and calling to him, the monitor suddenly showed a heartbeat for about ten seconds before it went flat again. Even the paramedics thought they had him. He knew I was there and he let me know the only way he could. Betty had just given me confirmation.

"Yes, it makes sense. Thank you," I say.

"He wants you both to know that he loves you and that he didn't want to leave you. This is what he was doing as he went into spirit:

"'Just one more minute. Just one more minute. Just one more minute.' That's what he was saying right before he passed into the light. 'Just one more minute. Just one more minute. Just one more minute.' He didn't want to say goodbye."

Okay. This is when Taliesin and I both lose it. The tissues we brought, just in case, are exhausted immediately.

Before we can get it together, Betty says, "May I approach you and your daughter?" I give her an affirmative nod because I can't speak. She motions for us to stand up and take a couple of steps forward. Once we're in place, she walks behind us and positions herself between us.

Then she wraps her arms around us on either side, and as she does, she brings the sides of our faces together until our cheeks almost touch and our bodies naturally tilt a little forward.

We hold this position as Betty tells us, "Your husband says, 'This is what we used to do.'" Then she releases us and returns to her spot in front.

I reach for Taliesin and she falls into my arms. This was our family hug. My husband's outstretched arms bringing the three of us together in a protective, loving embrace.

Elizabeth was right. Betty had not disappointed. It was the most remarkable reading I had ever received. It was a kind of healing for us. While our hearts were in pieces, somehow our spirits were a little lighter. And that made all the difference.

THE PEACE OFFERING

KATHLEEN HOLSTAD PEASE

Some of my memories are fading, but this one is clear as a bell.

The year was 1951 and I was four years old. I heard the solid metal jail door slam shut as I left the bedroom I shared with my parents and walked down the stairs to breakfast. Normally I heard voices coming up from the prisoners around our dining room table, but today there was only silence. I had overslept. The sun was shining through the window, which meant my two older brothers were already at school. I was confused by the stillness of the house.

I entered the dining room just as my father came through the open door that connected our county house with his office. There were two other doors in his workplace, one going to the courthouse next door and the other going outside, each with an etched glass window that read *Sheriff's Office*. He was carrying an empty metal tray. That meant he had taken the prisoners their breakfast, so no one would be eating with us this morning. That was unusual too. I was disappointed, since I liked to eat breakfast with Buffalo. He was one of our regulars. Each morning he would say, "Are you up to no good today, Kathleen?" That always made me smile.

My dad was the Rolette County Sheriff, which meant he was paid to maintain law and order in a North Dakota county consisting of four or five farming communities and the Belcourt

Indian Reservation, just seven miles from our town. Crimes in our county were usually drunken driving, disturbing the peace, or petty theft. My forty-two-year-old father was a stoic Norwegian, a second-generation American; a man of few words, but often when I entered the room, his upper lip, outlined by a pencil-thin mustache, would turn up on the ends and I'd get a wink that conveyed the love he couldn't put into words. He was a fit man; six feet tall and weighing less than 200 pounds. I thought he was very handsome in the gray fedora hat he seldom left at home. He had a good feel for his jurisdiction. I often heard him say, "Anyone can make a mistake and get into trouble."

Buffalo was a tall young man, a Chippewa Indian, with coarse black hair and a sculpted face. He often shared the breakfast table with us after spending a night in jail, and to me, he seemed to be almost a part of our family. I know my parents liked Buffalo too.

One night a few months earlier, as the wind was blowing and the snow was swirling in all directions, the lights in the house and jail went out. Dad was out on a call and Mom was in charge of the family and the jail. She said a fuse must have blown, and then she panicked. Her eyes were wide and darting around the room. The two-way radio that connected us to Dad in his car, and the furnace fan that kept us warm in this thirty-below-zero weather, were both dead. "I don't know where the fuse box is in this house or how to fix this," she said in a voice that was higher-pitched than normal, as she ran her hands through her hair.

There were several prisoners, including Buffalo, in jail that night, so she fumbled around in the kitchen until she found a flashlight, and then making her way to Dad's desk, found the jail key. She unlocked the massive door and called. "Buffalo!" He came out and she locked the door behind him. "I don't know where the fuse box is, Buffalo," she confessed. "It must be here in the office." She shined the light up and down over the walls until we saw the fuse panel. "I can fix this," said Buffalo in a reassuring tone that made my pounding heart slow down. He checked the fuses as Mom searched the bottom drawer of Dad's desk and found a box containing spare fuses. As Mom's shaking hands held the flashlight, Buffalo replaced the fuse.

Like magic, the two-way radio came to life, the room was bright, and the furnace fan whirled. Life as we knew it could continue. Mom took a deep breath and began to relax as she patted Buffalo on the back and said, "You saved the day, Buffalo. Thanks!" Buffalo nodded as Mom locked him back in jail. That Saturday, I heard my father talking to Buffalo. "I wish you could stay away from booze," he said. "It would make my job a whole lot easier and it would sure be healthier for you. After your night's sleep, you're a good guy to have around. Forget the Saturday night parties and just visit us when you're in town." Buffalo looked down at his plate and sighed as he said, "I can never seem to stop at one beer."

This morning, my dad was frowning and as I got closer to him, I was shocked to see red-streaked scrapes and bruises on his face and arm. He had a large scratch across his cheek and the skin around one eye was almost blue. "What happened to you?" I asked. Dad frowned and sighed and then said, "Last night I got a call that Buffalo was drinking and causing problems on the reservation again, so I drove out to pick him up, and he wasn't in the mood to cooperate. He was swinging his arms and caught my face, and the next thing I knew we were on the floor wrestling. He's in jail now, so you might say I won, but when I looked at my face in the mirror this morning, I wasn't sure. On top of that, in the scuffle, I lost one of my gloves."

As I looked at my dad's bruised face, I couldn't believe Buffalo would do that. For the first time, I realized my father had a dangerous job. In the excitement of his election and the move to this big house, I had never thought of anyone hurting him. Roy Rogers and Gene Autry dealt with criminals all the time in the movies and they never got hurt. In the constant pull of good versus evil, didn't the good guys always win? Buffalo was our friend. How could he hit my dad?

A few hours later, I was in Dad's office when an agitated, tired-looking Indian woman flung the door open and stormed in. She was furious. She had long, thick gray hair and fire in her eyes. She exploded, "You don't know me, but I am Buffalo's mother. You called him a 'son of a bitch' last night, and I am NOT a bitch!" I didn't know what 'son of a bitch' meant, but I could tell it wasn't good. She continued with, "No one calls me that!" My father's bad night was turning into his bad day. My stomach started to churn and my hands were sweaty as I watched from the office door while Buffalo's mother pointed her finger at my dad.

He sat down in his desk chair, looked up at her and paused. He let out his breath slowly and said, "You're right. I was angry and trying to control your son, but I didn't mean to insult you." He let out another tired breath and looked directly at her through his bruised eye and said, "I'm sorry!" The little office was suddenly silent. It seemed like the whole world was standing still as I watched Buffalo's mother, wondering what would happen next. She paused and slowly nodded her head, accepting his apology. Then she turned and calmly walked out of the office with her head held high.

Time passed and eventually things returned to normal between my father and Buffalo. My father had other cases to solve, and soon Buffalo had regained his seat at our table. Winter was truly upon us. Snowdrifts were almost door high in some places, and we all spent as much time as possible in the house. We were putting up our Christmas tree and my mother was baking cookies. The house was filled with the sounds of Bing Crosby dreaming of a white Christmas.

The day before Christmas, my father returned to his office from a meeting in the courthouse to find a package on his desk. It was wrapped in blue and silver paper that had seen many Christmases before. My father picked it up and put it under the tree. On Christmas morning, we had the usual early-morning rush to see what Santa had brought. When the excitement died down, my brother Gary found the blue and silver package and handed it to my father. He opened it, read the note, and smiled as he said, "Well, I'll be damned." It was a pair of black, fur-lined leather gloves, something dear to anyone spending a winter in North Dakota. Attached to the gloves was a small note written in irregular, block letters that said,

To the best Sheriff.
From Buffalo

WHEN SLEEPING WITH STRANGERS WAS SAFER THAN CHURCH

KM MCNEEL

I was warned I would be a walking menstrual threat while traveling in Egypt, untouchable. But I didn't flinch.

As a Texas gal, I was used to being seen as suspect. Though my feminist side tried to fight it, my upbringing had served me with a lifetime of longing for men's approval, along with a slice of cowgirl. A promising new job overseas as a communications officer to unify diverse Christian groups was my chance to saddle up and see the world.

My employer, the International Council on Church Unity, would send me to the same places they had sent my male predecessor, Robert. They foresaw no problem with my being a young female journalist. It was the late 1980s, after all.

I was to report on and photograph small-scale development projects globally that promoted liberal ecumenical Christian ideals, including helping the poor and refugees and supporting women's equality and gay rights. I also had to meet our hosting church dignitaries from any of the hundreds of member churches, follow their schedules, and dress primly but with style. The few of us who were women were to appear in local communities to encourage our sisters around the world.

From my first day in the Middle East, I was thrown into a new reality. Traveling to Egypt, I stopped to write up a regional peace conference on the divided island of Cyprus. There, one diminutive female was rounding up male priests and religious patriarchs from Syria, Israel, Cyprus and Turkey like a horse whisperer taming a herd of wild stallions. Justina Najjar, a Palestinian Quaker woman, quietly got these men to be cooperative and vulnerable. *And* she was my roommate! Well, we were the only women there.

At night, holding herself erect in carmines and saffrons, she prepared me for my next stop, in Egypt. Like an elder teaching an eager young chick her secrets, she leaned in.

"Don't even brush against any men from the Egyptian churches—or anywhere here in the Middle East. You see, you could be unclean from bleeding and revile them." She paused. "You know. Your period. Menstruation ...." She glanced around, as if the mere mention of "periods" would bring a menstrual sheriff to clap her in irons.

"Even in *Christian* churches?" I had asked my new friend. "Even if I'm not having my period?"

"Yes, of course," she chuckled. "They can't tell by looking."

When we parted in Cyprus, Justina's last words as we embraced were, "Remember what I said about touching!" With a smile she added, "Be you."

The minute my plane landed in Cairo, I was on show. It was a religious holiday and my hosts at the Coptic Orthodox Church had me meeting with religious luminaries like the Egyptian pope. But none of them were women. And that meant careful touch-free greeting. My Christian hostel, too, was staffed entirely by men who stared at me. I wanted to disappear.

I was desperate. Next morning, I searched my pocket guide for Western hotels with swimming. Cairo wasn't only a desert of moisture. I needed San Antonio pool life: bathing suits, white-nosed lifeguards. Flirtations. The Cairo Hilton was surrounded by a ten-foot wall. I would go there.

Once in the water, I did laps.

I hardly noticed the beautiful people swanning around above pool level until finishing up and "Ciao Bella" interrupted my musings. A well-manicured masculine hand offered me a lift. "My name is Armando," he crooned. "You are working in Cairo …?"

"Yes." I started toweling off, still loving the touch of his fingers on my wrist. "But our headquarters are in Switzerland." I tried not to stare at his physique while I told him about my work bringing different progressive groups together and hoped the churchy talk would put him off. I had to prepare for work the next day—Easter Sunday.

"I'm Swiss boy!" he said delightedly. "We dine tonight. And if you are a church girl, you will need something to wear."

I was astonished when later Armando gave me a hot pink dress with his offer of dinner, complete with matching shoes. When I untied the ribbon from the box it stopped me—just the designer fabric itself. He must have watched every movement while I was in the water because it fit perfectly. His attentions were intoxicating.

"Ciao, Ahmed," he said later to the headwaiter as we entered the restaurant of chandeliered tables. When we sat, Armando spoke of his apartments in St Moritz, Lake Como, "And one on Mont Blanc you can see from your offices, Bella." I tugged at the silky sleeves and waist of the dress to show less cleavage. A mushroom dish was so thrilling that I practically swooned—but that may have been the champagne.

Everything in the Christian hostel seemed perilous compared to his hotel room. His walls were a light lemony shade and all the fixtures and furniture were bone. Our lovemaking anchored me in this place of so many rules and terrifying consequences. He called me "Bella" all night, "*Beautiful*."

I started to drift in the afterglow, knowing I had work in a few hours. Hesitating till the last possible moment, I whispered, "Armando?"

He didn't stir.

"Armando, I have to go."

I forced myself away, dressing in my old clothes.

As I walked slowly toward the door, his fingers sort of flickered. "Ciao, Bella," he said without opening his eyes. He had called me only "Bella" all night.

Did he even remember my name?

It was surreal to reenter the hostel. I immediately felt guilty about indulging in the opulence of the Hilton. There was an invitation waiting for me, a special "fasting banquet" before Easter Sunday ceremonies at an Orthodox cathedral.

After a four-hour drive and a brimming vegan meal, my host, the idealistic Bishop Athanasias, escorted me and burst open his cathedral doors. He gestured me through as if I were the decorated family Christmas tree. I knew he was proud to be presenting a liberated, independent *Western woman* to his flock.

The smell and energy that greeted me were vaguely like a campfire after a Texas roundup. The intimate odors of working men mixed with exotic perfumes thickened the air of an enormous crowded dome. Several hundred, perhaps a thousand, men sat in the pews.

Looking up into the galleries and balconies, reaching one hundred and fifty feet toward the cathedral ceiling, I saw the Orthodox priesthood. Their gray hair hung down to their shoulders, touching the balcony rails, matched by their equally long beards. Opaque white trails of incense rose to make them appear as if they were hanging in clouds.

It took me a moment to realize I was the only woman in the place. *How could I avoid touching any of these men?* A white-clad nun mysteriously appeared to translate the daylong celebration for me. She escorted me to a well-hidden, marble-fenced area. There I found all the women.

I dove in, leaving the religious sister at the door. I could move in here without worrying about touching someone accidentally. My personal nun motioned me frantically to come back to the outer part where the men were. Then I started to realize it was an honor to wander into places usually reserved for men only. My work as a woman was to be a *pretend man.*

Soon Bishop Athanasias beckoned me forward with sweeping movements from far across the huge space. "A demonic beast from the Apocrypha," my nun was translating the readings. "It menaces Jerusalem."

From the raised central altar, the Bishop wanted me to come up the five steps, inside the holy gates, and photograph extreme close-ups at the altar. Center stage. I rose and started walking, feeling two thousand eyes on me. The crowds of men hushed.

When I approached, a young deacon at one side of the altar stared wildly, his white cassock shaking with emotion. The dignity of his golden stole and vestments did not hide an animal fear.

The atmosphere was crackling. The deacon started to signal me to go back. Then he took a step toward me, eyes now fierce, hands up as if ready to push. Oblivious, Bishop Athanasias continued to wave me forward, wanting a teachable moment against the stigma of menstrual blood.

I was expected to go on, "gunz-blazin'"-feminist-cowgirl style. Looking at the two men and feeling the tense energy surrounding me, I remembered the lessons of horse whisperers who know to turn away when animals are excited. That is why Justina told me not to touch men. So they would stay calm. It was compassion. How could they overcome two thousand years of indoctrination in an instant?

I took my aisle seat next to the nun. Both the young deacon and I breathed. The beast receded to the shadows in the text. I felt more learning took place without the inevitable confrontation, had I continued up those steps.

It was only in the tradition-bound confines of the ancient religions that the menstrual taboo was so limiting. In the next days outside the actual church walls, I was able to visit and record stories of many efforts in Cairo and meet dynamic women and girls.

And when I saw Armando again I asked him to call me by my name. Which, you know, he did.

CONFESSION OF A FATHERLESS SON

RICHARD FARRELL

Six months. That's all it took to turn my already unnerving childhood completely upside down in ways I'm still trying to unravel almost sixty years later.

I was fifteen when my parents died only six months apart. It was 1960, and I was a freshman in high school in Naperville, Illinois, about thirty miles west of Chicago, then a small farm town, now an exclusive suburb.

Looking back, I feel like I had a mom. I am the product of Corrine Farrell, a stay-at-home mother who was available, accepting, and loving. I can't say the same for my father. I do not feel I had a dad. George Farrell was largely absent from my life—either staying late at work in Chicago or at some sports event with his buddies there. When he did come home, he could be drunk and abusive and even more so as I reached my teens.

Yet, I see parallels between our two lives. Ties that bind us to this day. I am not here to blame my father but to put the finishing touches on understanding him.

My father died from internal bleeding after driving his car off the road on the way home from work. He was probably drunk. He often was. As I got older, I had paid closer attention to his condition when he entered the front door. The drunker he was, the more likely there would be a fight with my mother. And it could be awful.

My earliest memories were of happier times. From what I can tell through family stories, Mom and Dad had a grand life before my two brothers and I came along. My favorite photo of them shows Dad sitting on a bench with Mom on his lap in a dress, kicking up her heels, both with smiles as big as they come. It must have been around 1938, when they would have been in their late twenties. Then we came along. First my brother Don, then me six years later, and George ("Skip" to us) two years after.

From what I can recall, things were good when I was four, and my dad had a used-car lot next door to our home. It was successful enough for us to drive around in a nice-looking Cadillac and spend time at a summer cottage in Wisconsin. I don't recall strife between my mom and dad back then. Those were the good times.

Then a recession came, car values plummeted, and Dad had to close the lot. First, he became a salesman for a large auto dealer and was doing well. But then he wanted to be his own boss, so he teamed up with a buddy who had a used-car lot much farther away, in Chicago. That made for a long, often slow, commute, and as the years passed, he would sleep more and more often in the car lot.

After those early years, I had little connection with my dad. It was like he was a frequent visitor who sometimes misbehaved, whom I never quite felt comfortable with, and whom I skirted when I could. Financially, it was always a struggle in the years to come.

When Dad came home, my mother would often bring up money issues or the fact she wanted him around more. I didn't, but she did. The drunker he was, the worse it got. I never saw him hit Mom, but his words could cut like a razor. When in a rage, he might spit out, "Eat my shit." And he'd yell it over and over again while I lay in bed with a pillow over my ears, praying to God to take him away.

It is not like Dad did anything with us, even though Mom tried to encourage a connection. One time, Mom got my father to play catch with me. It was the only time I can ever recall my father and I doing anything together, just the two of us. And I mean ever. I pretended to have fun, but it felt awkward, and we never did it again.

Again at Mom's urging, my dad took my younger brother and me to one White Sox game and one Blackhawks hockey game. There were also a few trips to Arlington Park where Dad and his drinking buddies would gather to bet the horses.

Dad's anger got worse over the years, so by the time he died, I mostly felt relief. In the moment, I did not know the anger at him that would fester and follow me all my life.

The shock of losing my mother six months later was compounded by the fact that I was the one that found her. She had just come home from a party. I was in the bathroom brushing my teeth, and she was getting ready for bed in her bedroom close by, allowing us to chat with each other. But then she didn't respond to something I said, and I sensed something strange, feeling a mixture of fear and excitement. When I walked into her room, she was draped across her bed; half undressed, her legs, still in nylons, splayed and her face contorted, choking for breath. I ran to the phone and called for an ambulance and sat frozen where I was, too scared to go back to her room.

These disconcerting events left repressed feelings that were only felt years later with a therapist. First, in my 30s, I faced my anger at my dad as I was struggling with depression. Then, when I was 60, I dug up my guilt at deserting Mom when she was dying. The therapist lightened my burden by reminding me of how forgiving I had portrayed my mom and asking, "Do you really think she would blame you, her fifteen-year-old son, for hiding away in fear?" Funny how a few words can completely change the way you feel.

You might be asking at this point: What is the purpose of all this rehashing of the distant past? I am seventy-two and working on what I call the end game of my life. Trying to live whatever time I have left free of delusion and festering wounds. Most of it is not "work." Most days, especially when I feel down, I ask myself, *How can I have some fun today?* Usually, I can. It's mostly up to me. But as I think about Dad, I realize he is one wound that has not healed, so I'm revisiting my childhood in hopes of finding a more complete peace.

That's what I'm doing with my end game, trying to complete my life. Despite all the time I've had, I haven't been all that productive, which leaves me plenty of things to do: lots of sorting and loose ends to tie up, including writing more. And making peace with my past.

I am fairly at peace with my dad because I see more clearly how I am like him. I too have a lot of bar buddies and love watching sports. Also, I've spent half my working life in the field of horse racing, mostly as a writer for a handicapping publication, but also as an assistant in the Del Mar racing office. I think the latter is more coincidence than anything, but you know how some say there are no coincidences.

What I know is that my dad and I both have had the same need to feel free. For him, it was to be his own boss. For me, it has been the freedom to search for my unique way to contribute to society, to produce fruits uniquely my own. Perhaps it's the male counterpart to a woman wanting a baby.

Can't say I've produced much yet, but my end game is centered on that. And I have the presence of the ultimate deadline looming to keep me focused. I need deadlines. I'm the kind of guy who waits to pack for a trip until I fear I don't have enough time left to do it and make the plane.

Neither my dad nor I could stand being bound by the need for money or financial security if it cost us our freedom. The big difference is he didn't realize what he was, didn't realize that the great life he had with Mom before we kids came along could all change.

Recently, I heard someone say, "The words 'adult,' and 'easy' do not belong in the same sentence." I want an easy life, and so did my dad. More than once in my life, I've heard the sarcastic question, "So what are you going to do when you finally grow up?" Now I'm okay with it. I accept the likelihood I never will.

Having a family is not easy. You may have guessed by now I have never married or had children.

My father taught me well.

TATTERED FLAG

PHILIP PRESSEL

On the wall in my home office, in a frame measuring twenty by twelve, floats a tattered flag. Three vertical stripes of fabric stitched together: blue, white, red. There is a special cross in the middle of the white stripe: General Charles de Gaulle's Cross of Lorraine, the symbol of the Free French Army. The cross is barely visible, but I know it's there—because I drew it with a blue crayon the day after my mother gave me the flag. She'd had to leave me—again—with the family that was sheltering me from the bombing. I was seven, and liberation was near.

Other than a few letters from my father, this tattered flag is the only memento I have from my childhood in France. Every time I look at it, heartache and fear come rushing back. It isn't a medal, a symbol of a brave achievement; it's a reminder of war in a child's life. Separated from my parents, wondering if I would ever see them again, the loneliness I felt haunts me to this day.

I was born in Antwerp on June 22, 1937, the only child of Joseph and Miriam. When the Germans invaded Belgium on May 10, 1940, my parents, like so many others, had only time to grab one suitcase—and me—before crossing the border into France, headed for Marseille, hoping to get to the United States.

We did not make it. We wound up in Lyon, and then Paris. From 1940 to 1942, my father wrote letters to an uncle in New York asking for help, each letter more desperate than the last, until outgoing mail was no longer permitted. On September 28, 1944, three weeks after Lyon was liberated, my father wrote this:

> *Dear Uncle Eli,*
>
> *Ils vivent encore,*
>
> *Yes, we are still alive and can finally breathe in freedom.*
>
> *We feel like survivors of a cataclysm. The joy of feeling free is profound, but we worry about those dear to us whose fate is unknown, and we have seen too much suffering for this joy to be complete.*
>
> *For the past two years, human life counted for nothing. We waited for so long, and so fervently hoped for deliverance. Under mandatory order, our son, Phillipe, was evacuated last May in order to be sheltered from the bombings. The essential thing is that we can announce to you that we are safe and sound, and together.*
>
> *We have heard from Belgium that my in-laws are alive. My mother was deported in 1942, and I have not heard about her fate; my sister and her husband were also taken in 1942 to "a destination unknown." Will I ever see them again?*
>
> *Hoping that we soon receive detailed news from you, we send you our best wishes and kisses.*
>
> *Yours, Jos, Miriam, and Philippe*

At age seven, I was separated from my parents by edict that all children must be evacuated to the countryside. A wonderful Catholic family, the Sabathiers, took me into their home. They had a son my age named Jean. I lived with them in a small village seven miles south of Lyon for months, and though they were kind, I was a sad, frightened, and homesick little boy. My parents came to visit a few times, but at each farewell there were tears in all of our eyes, not knowing if this might be the last time we held each other close. In truth, I cried every night. I had a constant, immense feeling of constriction in my chest.

Unbeknownst to my parents at the time, the little town of five hundred people was one of the headquarters for the French underground, the Maquis, and so I remained in danger and continued to experience many frightening events, without the comfort of my parents.

From the hills around the town, the Maquis harassed the German troops, sniping at them with high-powered rifles as they passed through the valley.

The Germans responded with vicious reprisals. One afternoon, Jean, Mrs. Sabathier, and I were sitting in the dining room when we heard the ominous rumble of trucks and armored carriers approaching. We peeked through the dining room curtains at the scene unfolding in the town square below us. I stood to the right side of one window, behind the wall, trying not to be seen. An open truck filled with German soldiers manning four machine guns entered the square in front of the church. The machine guns were aimed in all four directions. Several armored cars and marching troops wearing those horrible German helmets followed them.

I could hardly breathe. We did not make a sound. It was the most frightening moment of my life. I remember the thundering noise the trucks made as they rolled through the town and the thumping of boots on the pavement. I wrapped my arms around myself to keep from trembling. Mrs. Sabathier put one of her arms around me—her touch calming, but not enough. I longed for my parents. The Germans crossed the square and continued down one of the side streets. A minute or two passed, the motors became quiet, and then we heard the staccato blasts of machine gun fire.

A few minutes later, the shooting ceased. The rumble of the trucks echoed through the valleys and then faded into the distance. When we were sure the Germans had gone, we went out, and we saw about a dozen villagers lying dead in the side street—men, women, and children. There was a smell of burned gunpowder and smoke. I can still see in my mind the image of the bodies and hear the sounds of crying that broke the silence. Innocent villagers mowed down in reprisal for the Maquis' actions. The Germans wanted to prove that resistance was futile, but they failed to stop it.

After D-Day, June 6, 1944, and the liberation of France, the Maquis were no longer afraid of reprisals. Their guerilla warfare intensified. One day, the Maquis caught two young German soldiers, stragglers from a convoy that had gone through the valley. The Maquis shot the young Germans on the spot. Jean and I, both only seven, went down to the field with some of the men from our village. We saw the German boys lying on the ground face up. Then some of the villagers unbuttoned their flies—and urinated on the bodies. Some months earlier, I'd taught myself to urinate silently, afraid that the noise would be heard. Standing there in that field, I was overwhelmed by the sight, the smell—and the sound. Even as a boy, I knew what it meant.

Relief became joy as the liberation progressed. The American troops coming up from North Africa came directly through our valley. I went down with other townspeople to wave and cheer for the American troops as they went by. I waved the flag my Maman had made for me, and the American soldiers threw Hershey bars at us. I will never forget it.

Soon after, I was reunited with my parents. Embracing them, walking with both their hands in mine, I was no longer alone. We had survived.

Years have passed. My parents are gone. But I look up at the wall in my office, and I see my tattered flag. And I remember that I, too, bear the marks of time, and I carry the memories of fear and loneliness and then, love and freedom.

BUTTERFLY KISSING LIFE

MARIJKE MCCANDLESS

The encounter was unforgettable, mystical, otherworldly. *What did it mean?* I ponder, sitting at my computer four months later. My mind spins and questions: *Was the butterfly a shamanic spirit animal helping and guiding me?* I Google "symbolism of butterfly encounter." I want someone else to divine the meaning of being kissed by a butterfly for an unfathomable thirty long … still … exquisite … sweet … blissfully carefree and innocent … minutes, while on a silent retreat last April.

I almost wish I'd imagined it or exaggerated it, so I could shy away from the impact of the experience, the truth of what had happened. Telling the story—even now, writing it down—I doubt myself, and I wonder if people will judge me and discount the accuracy of the telling, giving me a kind of out from accepting the full glory of the gift. But here's the thing: I unwittingly voice recorded it, all thirty-plus minutes of an extended encounter with a butterfly.

It happened. I participated.

At the time, I was on an eight-day silent retreat at the Zen Monastery Peace Center in Murphy, California, in the western foothills of the Sierra Nevada. This particular retreat included a combination of sitting meditation, working meditation, and personal time. All activity was done in silence. We were encouraged to honor "the privileged environment," which meant keeping deeply to oneself, avoiding not only speaking but even eye contact with others. Though my husband and I were both participating, we slept in different places and didn't talk to each other, accepting it as an opportunity for the inner personal work of spiritual transformation.

On this day, solo day or "holy leisure" day—the day during which there would be no instruction and no group meetings—I had fallen into a deep attitude of reverence while meditating in the temple. The attitude was marked by a willingness not to "know" anything. I felt humbled and inspired to approach all with awe, perhaps even trepidation, to be small before the greatness of existence, to be submissive to the overwhelming love from the divine that seemed to be present; to allow even suffering to take a backseat. I was this close to … to what? To something unknowable—something that might be called the source of life.

As I sat in the temple, it dawned on me the space for worshiping need not be limited to this sacred space. Rather, all of life was a cathedral. I got up and ventured outside.

My journey took me down a little trail through the forest. Nature was calling—in the form of a full bladder—and I was seeking an available outhouse. They all appeared to be occupied, so I kept on walking, turning on my phone's voice recorder to capture my musings.

We had been instructed to record moments of appreciation. On that day, full of gratitude, I was keeping a running commentary on the recorder. I noticed the clover lining the pathway and remembered being a small child searching for four-leaf clovers. I spoke into the recorder about my childhood love of magic and mystery and my current appreciation for the clover and the memory it invoked. Down the trail I noticed a butterfly on the ground just in front of me.

Oh sweet! my inner voice exclaimed in delight. I squatted slowly, watching with pointed focus, talking to it, praising it. My recorder was still on, capturing not only the silent gaps as the butterfly and I shared the same space, but also my small gasps of surprise and my quiet voice talking aloud to the butterfly. "You are beautiful," I whispered. In a bit, the butterfly turned and made its way toward me and then hopped up on my right hand. I watched, mesmerized, practically holding my breath, as the butterfly extended its long, spiraled tongue and then kissed my hand all over—taking many minutes to cover the entire backside of my right hand.

Then, beyond reason or expectation, the butterfly hopped to my left hand and kissed it all over too.

What was this?

The encounter had now extended five to ten minutes—longer than any reasonable hope. Confounded but present, I watched as the butterfly flew from my left hand to land on the backside of my left shoulder, encouraging me to turn my head to look at it. I watched as it gently flew to the ground behind me and hopped in four-inch increments the other way.

Ah, that was wonderful, I thought, pivoting on my squatting legs to face it, before slowly beginning to stand. But then, the butterfly took flight again and landed back onto my right hand, staying with me as I stood. I took a tentative step. The butterfly remained. I began walking back the way I'd come, but this time with the butterfly on my hand all the while, as I continued recording my murmurings of awe and appreciation.

The butterfly and I walked together back up the trail for another ten minutes or so. There was not a thought in my head. My being was mesmerized and focused, reverent, and so quiet. The recorder captured only the sounds of my footsteps.

Then as I passed by my husband, Jay's, hermitage (a tiny one-person rustic hut in the woods), my attention flittered and a thought popped in: "I want to share this with Jay!"

This thought was immediately followed by the recollection this was not allowed on the silent retreat, even for husband and wife, and yet I was tempted. I turned toward the pathway to his hermitage, and as I did, the butterfly flew away to a nearby tree.

"Oh!" I said aloud.

I immediately recognized my lapse in attention, saw myself grasping for something other than this precious moment, not trusting its inherent perfection, but subtly seeking to improve it. I stopped. I let go of my desire to see Jay, looked at the butterfly on a nearby tree branch, and approached. "Please accept my apology," I murmured. "I'd like to continue with you."

The butterfly flew back onto my hand and we continued walking up the trail, together.

Another five or ten minutes passed. I noted someone was coming down the trail but kept my eyes downcast as encouraged while on retreat.

All of sudden there was a loud noise in the bushes immediately to my right—a crashing sound that the recorder captured. An enormous antlered buck sprinted away, feet from me.

The sound startled me and I looked up. So did the person heading my way.

It was Jay.

Our eyes caught. We both saw the deer. Shockingly, the butterfly remained on my hand, despite the noise.

The moment, though brief and unintended, was shared after all. Jay and I did nothing further, lowering our eyes and passing quietly. I couldn't even be sure he'd seen the butterfly on my hand, though after the retreat he confirmed that he had.

The butterfly and I continued on another five or ten minutes. As we approached the dorm, I became aware again of my still-full bladder. At the intersection with the door that led to inside bathrooms, the butterfly flew away.

I was grateful, for nature (of a different sort) was definitely calling. I glanced down at my recorder and turned it off, noting thirty-five minutes had passed. I went inside to relieve myself. When I came back outside, a (*the?*) butterfly flew directly in front of my face and then left.

I turned and headed back down the path toward the outdoor shower, and as I stepped on the earth with complete mindfulness, it dawned on me that I was walking on God's hand, just as the butterfly had been walking on me—each step probing and appreciating the earth.

I reflected that I'd just had a profound "life cathedral" experience with a butterfly, immediately followed by mundane simple activities: going to the bathroom and taking a shower; things I might have spiritually discounted before. Taken as a whole, they create a beautiful sustainable resonance, like breathing. And each—mystical butterfly encounters and ordinary daily activities—are both potent opportunities to let go of what I think needs to happen and instead pay attention to what *is* happening.

Now, these many months later, having freshly listened to the recording while writing this, instead of wondering about the significance of the singularly memorable butterfly encounter, I ask myself, *What is more important: the extended moment when a butterfly is kissing me all over, or the moments when I am the butterfly kissing life all over?*

I don't know.

But I appreciate this: the butterfly and I come from the same source; each a child of this universe. And I don't really need Google to confirm a natural understanding that the butterfly symbolizes transformation—a complete annihilation of one thing (the caterpillar) in order for the next thing (the butterfly) to arise. So, I invite the questioning, doubting small self, the one seeking the approval of others, the one trying to control life—the one who first sat down to write this article—to be exposed, to be annihilated. I close my computer and look within for the stillness and reverence of this moment, the one I am experiencing right now: cluttered desk, typing fingers, program management "to do" list calling. As I stop paying attention to the swirling thoughts, I see there is humility, reverence, magic, and awe right here, right now. I metaphorically bow before my messy desk, appreciating it too.

I am encouraged to revisit my butterfly recording and other recordings, along with my journal entries written during spiritual retreats, because in them I often have captured innocent uncalculated moments of gratitude and unknowing, reminding me of the bounty and abundance present in any moment whenever I leave my grasping mind behind—the one perpetually trying to improve life—and instead simply stop, pay attention, and kiss life all over.

NOT A DRILL

SARA MOHTASHAMIPOUR

FORT WORTH, TEXAS – 2004

I am just settling in at my desk at First Command Financial Planning after lunch, wishing for a nap. I hear it first, and then it crawls up my fingertips and down my spine. The sound echoes in my ribcage and drills deep in my soul, uprooting layers of darkness, memories, and denials.

I close my eyes, but it doesn't help. *Wait! Am I breathing?* I don't think I am. Who knew you could hold your breath for so long and not die? Who knew a fire alarm could teleport you back eighteen years and twelve thousand miles in an instant?

UrrrRRRRRRRRrrrrrr UrrrRRRRRRRRrrrrrr

TEHRAN, IRAN – 1986

I am sitting in a classroom with thirty other eight-year-old girls. Our teacher is writing on the blackboard. She has white chalk dust all over her black uniform and scarf, but I can't see what she is writing. There are too many heads between the front of the class where the board is and me.

Our classroom used to be a bedroom of an apartment just a short few years ago. Before the war. Before the revolution. Before any of us studying in it now was born.

Our desks weren't designed for three kids, either. There is so little space that we have to fold our notebooks in half so we can get three of them on the desk. No room for elbows. No room for extra pencils or an eraser unless you can keep them on top of your notebook as you write.

And I am trying, really trying, to focus, but I can't see the board. Also, my backpack is by my feet, and I'm worried that I'm going to step on it and get mud all over it and have more points deducted from my Ethics grade. *I can't lose any more points!*

Two weeks ago, I had forgotten to cut my nails short and was deducted a point. This morning, I was caught talking to my friend, Neda. Mrs. Naini, our principal, had been talking about regional inspections. Warning us to be "extra careful and not let a single hair slip out of our scarves" or else the inspectors would deduct points from our school's Ethics grade.

I was listening to Mrs. Naini, I really was, but I also had to show Neda my pretty new eraser. It was pink with orange circles all over it and smelled like gum and cotton candy. I had waited months to buy it and just had to show Neda before class and—I got caught. And my nails were long again. *Three points gone in two weeks!*

And now I can't see the board, and my backpack probably looks like a giant glob of mud now, and …

UrrrRRRRRRRRrrrrr

Then a man's voice: **"Attention! Attention! The siren you are now hearing is to announce danger or a red situation. And it means air strikes are on their way. Leave where you are immediately and seek shelter."**

We all know what it means, but no one moves.

With a shaking hand, I reach over the desk, take the pink-

and-orange eraser off my notebook and, as slowly as I can, put my hand in my pocket. Afraid my smallest movement may give our location away to THEM.

TEXAS

"Okay, girls, we gotta go," M, our manager, says, so calmly she almost sounds bored. "Our floor team captain is a total jerk; let's go, girls!"

Seek shelter! Seek shelter! The voice echoes in my head, but I can't move. I feel M's hand on mine and jerk it away. She holds up both her hands in surrender.

"What is that? That sound! What the hell is that?" My voice is clawing its way up my throat.

"It's a fire alarm; it's a drill."

"What the fuck is a drill? Is the building on fire?" I make fists to keep my hands from shaking.

"No, silly." She lets out a laugh. "It's *in case* there is a fire, we all know what to do. Don't forget your phone. This could be boring."

TEHRAN

"Okay, girls, the air strikes are closer today; leave everything here and quickly and quietly follow me."

Everyone starts running out the door. We are quick but not quiet. I half walk/half get pushed out into the hallway. Kids are pouring out of classes and toward the stairs from every corner. Teachers and staff are trying to guide us. The screechy noise hasn't stopped. Some kids are crying. Our teachers look like they want to cry. We keep moving. We take the stairs down to the first floor, and down to the garage, and BOOM!

The ground shakes, and we all let out a sound closer to a whimper than a scream. A huge frame with the picture of the Supreme Leader falls off the wall; the glass shatters, and this time, everyone screams. We start walking again, but faster now. I see a little girl standing in the corner against the wall crying, the front of her pants slightly darker than the rest of her uniform.

TEXAS

"Have y'all tried this new flavor? It's nasty!" S says, spooning Yoplait's newest flavor, *Raspberry Lemonade,* in her mouth as she walks down the stairs at a leisurely pace. "Hey! Did you bring cigarettes?"

UrrrRRRRRRRRrrrrrr – UrrrRRRRRRRRrrrrrr –

Yogurt? What does that matter, if we're all dead? Walk faster! Walk faster! The stairwell feels narrower and darker and hotter as we descend.

TEHRAN

"Away from the windows!" I recognize Mrs. Naini's voice. Everyone has started running. More kids are crying. The floors are wet. We grab each other, too afraid to fall. Too afraid to stop, to slow down.

I'm running with one hand in my pocket, tightly holding on to my eraser. We finally get to the basement where the school's janitor lives. His home is an almost-empty room. BOOM! The ground shakes, I close my eyes, and I feel heat behind my eyelids. BOOM! BOOM! BOOM! We jump in unison with every bomb. I shut my eyes tighter, trying to pretend it's just thunder and lightning. But it never rains when it's over. It smells like dirt and dust afterward.

Mrs. Naini shushes us, and everyone goes quiet. *Can they hear us up there? Is that how they find us?* I look around but can't see much besides girls in gray uniforms. It's dark, and I can smell fresh bread. There are over five hundred school children stuffed in a small basement, but it's the smell of bread that makes me panic.

My dad buys fresh bread every Friday morning for the weekend. Today is Thursday. *Will he still get fresh bread if I die today? What if they hit my brother's school and he dies? What if they hit our house and my mom and baby sister die?*

I want my sister, Sahar, to have the eraser if I die. She is only three years old; I must leave something for her to remember me by. *But how would they know where to find it? What if I get buried alive? What if they don't come looking for me?* My dad will know I am missing when he brings home fresh bread for breakfast tomorrow, and I am not there. *But what if he thinks I am outside playing with the kids? What if they never realize I am gone?* Sahar is gonna grow up not knowing she had a big sister. *I want my mommy! I wanna go home.*

TEXAS

We gather in the Forest Bank parking lot across from our office. People are laughing, joking, smoking. I find a wall a few feet from the crowd so there is something I could lean on. There is no point in trying to find shade. I let the Texas sun burn my skin. I surrender.

I look across the street at our building. Tall, whole, and strong. Tears burn a trail down my face and inside my blouse. It smells like summer and freshly cut grass and cigarette smoke. Not burned flesh, not dust, not gunpowder, not the metallic smell of death.

"Hey! D and I are going to leave early and grab a drink! I mean, we all need it after this, right?" I laugh with her and, for once, I am thankful for her self-involvement.

TEHRAN

"One at a time, girls. It's over now." Mrs. Naini is guiding us back up to our classrooms. The "code green" (all-safe siren) had been broadcast. No one had moved in that little basement until jolted by her voice. Back in our classroom, we sit in our chairs, barely moving. Our teacher continues teaching. We continue listening. And I continue not being able to see the board.

I walk home from school that day as I do every day. I hold my breath as I turn the corner and peek down my street. *My house is still there!* I run home and push the door open.

"There you are." My mom looks pale and tired. "How was school?"

"It was alright." I know better than to talk about today—to talk about "it." There is one thing no one does at home or school. We don't talk about the war.

My baby sister, Sahar, runs across the room. "What did you bring me?" she says in a singsong voice.

"Oh, I have a present for you!" I put my hand in my pocket. My throat goes dry, and my armpits sting.

"Let me see! Let me see!"

I pull my hand out of my pocket, and crumbles of pink and orange fall from between my fingers.

"What is that?" she says disappointedly.

I choke back tears "Look! It's confetti!" I throw torn pink and orange eraser pieces in the air. She squeals with joy.

INCEPTION

RUTH LAUGESEN

We move slowly from our table of Bloody Marys to the beach; five moms on the last day of a weekend escape. There's the water, turquoise and flashes of Garibaldi orange—a false tropical promise. The horizon's lemon-frosting smear masks Los Angeles. The headache is real. And yesterday, her mouth on mine was real.

The others give us space, their faces in phones. Liz and I sit a few feet apart in the sand. We broke code. It feels like everyone knows, at a molecular level. Even my husband, Damon, five beers in at a party weeks later, will shout, "What happened on Catalina? Look at you guys!"

Only yesterday we ran the 10K that gave us license to be here, dove in that frigid blue water, and gathered on couches in a peeling rental property to drink, to ramp up for the night; to suck on the marrow of our words.

"So, let's get down to it," I said. "What, or should I say who, are you into?" Drinks were sipped as each mind paused on the edge of vulnerability. One said, "I'm straight. I like boys. Lots of boys. My husband knows my MO."

Another confessed, "I'm not. I have many faces. The world sees what it needs to. I like women. I'm married but I'm all about women, always have been."

I said, "My husband asked ten years ago, before our wedding, 'Is this going to be a problem?' Talking about my occasional thing for girls."

Liz's comment is, "I don't mind guys; hell, I loved my high school boyfriend. I'm like a seven out of ten on the straight-lesbian spectrum. My ex-wife seemed like a ten out of ten. Got that wrong."

Liz had been with the same woman for twenty years. That woman just left Liz for a man.

Later she stands—lit by the sinking sun, in our bedroom doorway—shower damp in a small white towel and asks, "Do you mind?"

I turn to see skin where the cloth skims the top of her thighs. Only just below.

I say, "Not at *all.*" I'm thinking, *Oh, Jesus.*

"We roll naked a lot at our house," she explains, espresso eyes on me.

I say, "Fine with me," looking at the delicate shadowing under her collarbone. Perched on the bed we will share, I don't know what to do, but as the towel falls, premonition makes me move my night guard and earplugs to where she won't notice.

A few hours later and the bar is bamboo-backed booths and drinks that are tides of pink, red, and orange. The corners are indigo, the singer's mustache a curving black bridge.

There are younger, prettier women she flirts with, faces clean and lovely. But my arrogance comes five drinks in. Knowing my target and feigning freedom, I dance until her glances become stares. My movement is a call, arms stitching a complicated pattern of suggestion. It's pure chess.

I can smell her now; we're nearly touching. I want this. We are drunk; she is drunker. I run my lips and nose across, down her forehead, cheek, that neck, and pull away. Our hands clasp, my jeans scrape hers. We weave through lean, trucker-capped boys throwing it down. Our friends observe from above the rims of pint glasses. When she turns to talk to them, I panic and flee. Pushing through bodies, exploding past the bouncer, I run until the ocean stops me. Crying vodka tears, I ask the sea what I want. The waves persist, slurping at the shore, shapeshifting, indifferent. When I head back to the bar, Liz lifts an eyebrow, mouths, "Are you okay?" I shrug, and I drag her outside.

In salty darkness, hands move over ribs, fingers cling. The rawness of what I want makes me tremble. Leaning in, hair clouding us, she murmurs, "Are you in or out?"

"I don't know."

She takes a step back, her palm finds mine, and we walk instead toward the next pulsing beat.

But climbing the club stairs she exhales, fingers stopping my ascent. She says "Shit," grabs my arms, pushes me against the filthy wall. I taste the beer and her. The whole night is in her mouth.

Her mouth on mine. Finally on mine. And I freeze.

Not because I feel bad, or don't want to, but four wines, two vodkas and a beer in, I'm following the fucking script, every ounce of training in how to be a good girl but play the game. Deny your craving.

All I *want* is to cup her face.

Turning my head, I say, "I can't."

I want to take it back but she's already stepping away, saying, "I'm sorry, I'm drunk. I didn't mean to."

"Maybe we should go." She turns and walks back down the stairs.

Hands in pockets, we walk, cleaved, my action as irreversible as an ax through melon. Yet, at the door of the rental she asks one last time, "Is it him? He might not mind, you know. This doesn't have to go anywhere."

"I know, I know," I say, mind already there, how I'd say to Damon that I'm tired, that I don't know what's wrong.

In this kiss I have seen, and already forsaken, my life.

What I *want* is intimacy. And swaying drunk on the pavement, the cock of her head waiting, I already know I won't get it.

We find our bed in silence. I expect our bodies to ignore our words. But she sleeps facing away. And I am not brave enough to trace her moonlit shoulder.

I dream of her and wake exhausted. She turns to me at dawn. We do not touch.

Recalling countless sexual acts performed at the behest of too many men, I say, "This would've ended very differently if you were a guy."

Liz tries to smile, fails, and rolls to face the ceiling, "That's me, master of self-control." She closes her eyes.

Back home we sit on too many couches, not quite touching, an agony of potential. Her arms crossed, fists balled under her breasts.

She tells me, "I'm very attracted to you, but there's no good outcome to this."

What I want to hear is, "*Fuck* it," and be there when she loses control.

Instead, we bake cookies with the kids. She passes me sprinkles her buttered fingers can't open. "Excuse my slime," she says, smiling. I take the bottled blue stars, and a sweet ache I can hardly stand pulses in my folds.

She texts me: *You're very much on my mind today.*

I write: *I've never felt so conflicted.*

She replies: *Been losing sleep on this one.*

Even as her phone ripples with texts from the new online girl. She calls their dating "a classic case of redirected sexual energy."

Next time she texts to tell me about her: *She's from LA – super fun. I like her, hope that doesn't weird you out.*

I text back: *Just wish I was somehow part of your journey instead.*

She responds: *I get it. Please forgive me for creating this – I find you… intriguing. Doing my best to ignore. Circumstances not in alignment. As Erykah Badu says, next lifetime?*

A week later she's in bed with LA girl.

The disappointment is a lemon suckering in my mouth, an ache in my cheeks, a brick in my chest. These days will not be spent tasting her skin. They'll be spent uttering effortful words with friends, being a good-enough mom and wife, hiding the tornado inside.

I text back about my efforts with Damon and that I understand her choice. It's all cool. Waiting for her to realize her mistake.

She never does.

SINGLE RED LINE

DANIELLE B. BALDWIN

I couldn't tell if that single red line staring back at me was sullen or smug. It was the seventh I had seen in as many months, marching with slow determination across the display of a pregnancy test. It kept its composure as it darkened on the white background; far more than I could, as I held its housing in my shaking hands. *Please*, I thought to myself, *please tell me I'm pregnant.*

I tipped the test to one side and then to the other as my panic rose in my chest, its feathers brushing up against my ribs as it got ready to take flight. That wasn't something you were supposed to do—tip the display back and forth. The instructions were very clear that after putting the "absorbent tip" in your urine stream you are to leave it on a flat surface for two to three minutes. Closing my eyes, the good little girl I used to be, with my hair tightly pulled into the perfect pair of blue-marble-bound pigtails, wagged her finger at me for doing something I shouldn't have done. She was quickly replaced by the wilder, carefree version of that little girl, with her hair in knots and her fingernails dirty from spending all afternoon exploring in the woods. "Shake it again," she said.

But I couldn't help thinking that there was something wrong. Maybe one reason the red line hadn't twinned from a single to a double was that my pregnant pee, bursting with pregnant-lady hormones, hadn't made it all the way into the test. *Did I hold the test in my urine long enough? Maybe I had the tip pointed upwards in the stream (another pregnancy test no-no)? Could there be something wrong with the test? Just like a two-tailed coin, maybe this test was only capable of showing one line, no matter the circumstances. Maybe this was a bad batch?* My panic began to sweep against my entire chest, rattling hard to find an exit. I steeled myself against the rising tide of fear. I felt like if I let it out, it would suffocate me.

Truth be told, this was the second brand of test I had used. The first month, the choice felt simple. I casually looked at a few boxes, reading each of their claims on simplicity and accuracy, then chose a brand I had heard of, in the middle of the price range, with nice packaging, and threw it in my red plastic basket to keep my Advil and sunscreen company. I had originally chosen a test that indicated pregnancy with a plus or minus. Pregnant or not pregnant. Very simple.

The more tests that came back with a minus instead of a plus, the harder it was to face the minus. More accurately, the more difficult it was for me to face the lack of a plus. With every minus I was reminded of all the additions I was missing out on; the warmth of a baby sleeping on my chest, the tiny fist curling around my index finger, the beautiful blue eyes staring back up at me. I was not making any additions to the world or to my family. I wasn't getting more than the standard grade. I was a planner. A doer. A believer in Henry Ford quotes, like "If you think you can, you can. If you think you can't, you're right." And here I was, thinking I could, and it still seemed like I couldn't.

Instead, I kept getting minuses. They indicated I was less than, that I was subtracting from the world by my continued inability to get pregnant. Based on that test display, I was either an addition or a subtraction, helping or hurting, giving or taking away. For the first four months, I was never a plus. It was the absence of plus that sent me to the drug store for a new type of test. One that showed one line or two. And while the single red line was still technically a minus, it didn't seem as judgmental. One line compared to two seemed more humane. Until now. Now I was reminded that a minus was still a minus.

I had always thought that I would get pregnant quickly. My parents often told the story about how I had been a "surprise" conceived in a hotel in Florence while they were on vacation and my mother was on birth control. She was thirty-four at the time, had an eight-year-old and a five-year-old already, and had had several miscarriages. They were stunned to come back to the US and realize that their third child was on the way. Because I was also thirty-four, I assumed that the same "the wind blows and you're pregnant" circumstances would apply to me. So while Chris and I were starting later than my parents had, I still felt that the odds were in our favor.

I came across a picture not too long ago of my sixteen-year-old self, as I stood in the doorway of the Hotel Daniela, grinning at the camera with the excitement of a teenager standing below the sign that was her namesake. What was not captured on film was that smile as it melted into horror as I realized I was standing in the doorway of a hotel where my parents had sex.

Chris and I had decided to "pull the goalie" in June of that year. After the summer passed without us getting pregnant, I felt my first brush of panic and I went to see my doctor. Since doctors fix things, right? She assured me that after more than a decade of birth control, my body would need to adjust. It would need to shake off the shackles of hormone regulation, to regain its own rhythm as it jogged down the street under the trees, stretching its legs and building up its pace. The stress of my new job hadn't helped, adding hurdles and obstacles in the way. But these were starting to clear over the past few months. All we had was open road, and I felt ready.

We had done everything right. Chris and I had sex at exactly the right time, according to the ovulation test I had taken. I had cross-checked the days using a tracking calendar, and just to be sure, I had mapped my temperature using a basal thermometer. A few friends that were churchgoers said prayers. Others sent their thoughts, good energy, or big hugs. I meditated, exercised, and slept well. I had already started to follow the diet of a pregnant woman; no more nitrates, sushi, or alcohol. I had even taken the drastic step of kicking caffeine to the curb a few months back. It was a tough breakup. He grumbled and slammed the door on his way out.

I often thought about the showers, the registries, the nursery, and hopefully, the little baby girl that would allow me to start over. As a mom, I would mirror my own mother's creativity, her strength, and her heart. And I would put her selfishness, her need for drama, and her addiction in a box in the closet that my children would never see. And each month passed with a minus or just a single line on the pregnancy test.

I felt deep in my bones that this test result would look different than the others. This was the month that the display would have two lines instead of one. These past few days, my body felt different—fuller, more whole. My skin felt fresh, my hair thick. Those two lines would tell me that there were now two people in my body instead of just one.

But this test was no different. It had just one.

One.

Single.

Fucking.

Red.

Line.

And with that, my hopes of having a baby flatlined for the eighth month in a row.

FOURTEEN: A DAUGHTER'S MEMOIR OF ADVENTURE, SAILING, AND SURVIVAL

LESLIE JOHANSEN NACK

By the fall of 1973, nearing my thirteenth birthday, I transformed from a little twelve-year-old girl into a five-foot, six-inch curvy young woman. I hated seventh grade and dreamed about the day we'd take off sailing to exotic islands and could stop going to school altogether. Being only one year apart, Monica and I were in the throes of puberty together. Monica was tall—five-foot, eight inches—and skinny. Her breasts developed slowly and were A-cup sized. My breasts blossomed fast and soon were C-cups. Most people thought I was the oldest.

One day after we got off the school bus, I saw Dad talking to a man in the parking lot. "Hey, Leslie, come here a second," Dad yelled out.

Monica punched my arm lightly, smiled and said, "Bummer," and continued to our boat.

I walked toward Dad, watching his eyes travel up and down my body, as my sandals went flip, flip, flip. I looked down at my shoes, the most interesting thing in the world to me, trying to ignore him. I waited by his side as he finished up his conversation. We were taught never to interrupt, never! Children were to be seen and not heard—that was the motto in the Johansen family.

"Why do you wear your bathing suit top to school?"

I had on my blue-and-white-striped string bikini top under a white T-shirt. It was visible through the T-shirt and I thought it looked good—like I lived at the beach.

"I don't know. I like wearing it," I said.

"It looks like a bra to me," he said, "and my girls don't wear bras. Only pregnant girls need bras."

I stared at the pavement. "All the other girls at school have bras."

"All the other girls aren't my daughters. We are European, and European girls don't wear bras. Besides, you look beautiful without one—natural, like a young woman should look."

Across the parking lot, a surfer walked up from the beach, his wetsuit shining in the afternoon sun, carrying his board under his arm. I said nothing, knowing it was a losing battle.

"You're not shaving your legs or underarms, are you?" Before I could answer, he bent over and ran his hands up my shin, then lifted my arm to look underneath it.

"Good girl. Don't be like all the other girls. Be a Johansen. Be proud to be European." I spaced out, put up the invisible walls around me, the ones that had always protected me when he got too close into my space. My eyes looked ahead but everything around me was blurry, unfocused. I yearned for something I couldn't verbalize: the day my body was my own.

"You can go now. Get your homework done, then I have chores for you," he said.

He kept a close watch on me for the next few weeks, making sure I didn't wear my bathing suit top under my clothes. It became a game. I tried stuffing the tiny little string bikini top into my backpack, but he found it. I had no choice but to go to school feeling vulnerable and naked.

At school, every girl wanted to go steady with a cute tanned surfer, and I was no exception. One day as I walked out of the cafeteria, my breasts swaying with no bra, one of the guys on the wall yelled, "Hubba hubba. What's your name?"

I could hear them laughing. Using the same strategy I used when Dad leered at me, I put up my invisible walls, blurred everything out, and kept walking. I focused on the library. *If I can just get into the library I'll be safe*, I thought, and then someone hooked an arm through mine and walked fast, shielding me from the boys on the wall. It was Raine Oliver, the girl who sat next to me in homeroom. If I was a C cup, then Raine was a D, or maybe a DD. She was only five-foot-two, with long brown hair, freckles all over her face, and big brown eyes. Her boobs were way out of proportion for her little body, and as we walked arm-in-arm to the library, another of the boys yelled out, "Hey look, Balloons has a friend—Baby Balloons."

Raine and I became instant friends. I told her the story of how we weren't allowed to wear bras because we were European.

"Let's go shopping tomorrow. I know where we can get you a bra for free," she said.

The next day we ran the entire way to the D.A.V., a second-hand store run by the veterans, on Coast Highway. To my surprise, the bras were all in boxes on a shelf, and they were new. I took three different-sized bras into the dressing room and tried them on. They were all white with a little pink flower in the middle front. They felt confining and tight, but at the same time safe and secure. When I tried on the 36C, it felt right. I loved the bra and felt a surge of happiness. I left the bra on under my shirt as Raine instructed and skipped out with no problem.

When I got back to the harbor, I hid the bra, rolled up in a ball, on the ground behind the middle toilet in the boat-owner's bathroom because it seemed nobody used the middle toilet very often. The bathroom was the only private space Dad couldn't get to. It was my sanctuary. I checked on the bra twice the next day to make sure it was still there. On Monday morning, I put the bra on. I loved it. I swore Monica to silence, threatening her life.

A month or so later, asleep in the forward bunk with Monica, I woke up with a headache, clutching my stomach. I felt nauseated, with roaring cramps down low. The thin yellow morning light peeked through the porthole, and I could tell it was barely light outside. Rolling over, I felt something wet. I pulled the covers back and found blood. I yelled, "Oh no!" which made Dad come running from the aft cabin, where he was just getting up.

Dad stood over our bunk. "Ah, Leslie, goddamn it," he said as he looked at the mess. I shrunk back. "I guess I have to go the store and buy you some pads—just what I want to do at 6 a.m. on a Saturday morning."

"Sorry, Dad." I sank back into the cushions and pulled the covers over my head.

He turned and left the boat. "I'll be back with pads in twenty minutes!" he yelled.

The boat rocked as he stepped onto the dock, and I waited a few minutes for Dad to walk down the dock. "I'm sorry Monica, I really am."

Monica jumped out of bed. "It's okay, Leslie. Don't worry. I'll help you clean it up."

I changed pajama bottoms, grabbed the sheet and sleeping bag, and took them down the dock to the boat-owner's bathroom. I wondered what Mom was doing at that very moment—why she couldn't be there to help me. She was never there for the important stuff.

It was bright out, one of those cold, clear, late-fall mornings. The harbor was peaceful and still for a Saturday morning. I was grateful I didn't see anybody except the brown pelicans sitting on the end of the dock.

I got in the shower with the dirty linens, standing on the sleeping bag to keep my feet off the cold tile, and turned on the hot water. A lump grew in my throat as I stood in the steamy shower. Maybe it was the hormones, or the embarrassment of Dad seeing the bloody bed, but it was suddenly all too much. I couldn't stop the tears. They came in a flood, unlocking all the other pains I'd stuffed away. The well was deep and it scared me, because once I let some of it out, controlling it was impossible. The pain echoed off the cement walls, ricocheting around the bathroom as I cried about Mom, Dad's weirdness with me, the bra, and now this. I cried so hard I struggled to catch my breath, hiccupping between outbursts.

I couldn't tell anybody what had happened that morning or how humiliated I was once again. Everybody thought we had such a great life. We lived on a boat—how fun. We were going to sail around the world—how lucky. But I wished I lived in a house like all the other girls I knew, wished I didn't have to act happy about heading out into the open sea with Dad. I didn't want people to look at me and point. I wanted to blend in.

The bathroom door opened and then slammed shut. I stopped crying. Monica knocked on the shower door. "Leslie, I could hear you crying all the way down the sidewalk." I didn't say anything. "Take the belt and pads Dad got you."

"I don't want to wear that," I said.

"Why not?" Monica asked.

"Because I don't want to. I want to wear tampons."

"I don't think Dad would let you do that," she said.

Monica hadn't started her period yet, but I knew she was right. My pain hardened into anger. Anger at Mom for not being there, at Dad for yelling at me for starting my period, at everybody in the world who was so happy we were sailing around the world. Dad didn't scare me anymore. Letting those emotions out in the shower left room inside—room for some anger.

I reluctantly put on the stupid old-lady pad and shoved the sheet and sleeping bag in the washer. Filled with bravado, I stormed down the metal ramp, scaring the pelicans into flight. With each step I gained more courage. When I got to the boat, I found Dad making coffee in the galley. Monica had followed me down the dock and stood behind me as I boarded *Aegir*.

"I don't want pads. I want tampons," I said.

"What are you talking about? Young girls don't wear those!" he yelled.

"Yes, they do! How do you know, anyway?" I yelled back.

He stepped back against the gimbaled stove, looking a little surprised. Then he dug in. "Who wears them?"

"My friends. They all wear tampons."

"Raine? Raine wears tampons? I can tell she's that kind of girl."

"What kind of girl?" I asked with my hands on my hips.

"A girl that's easy."

"You don't know anything!" I screamed. "Raine's not easy! Stop talking about my best friend like that—I hate you!" I ran to the forward bunk and buried myself in Monica's sleeping bag. Dad laughed. "Ah, Leslie, misguided stupid little girl," he said. The boat rocked again as he stepped off, and the sound of his flip-flops disappeared down the dock. I buried my head in the pillow and screamed until my throat hurt. Monica had been sitting quietly in the main salon. "You really told him, Leslie," she said with a big grin. I picked my head up from the pillow. "Yes, I did. And I'll tell him again and again if I have to. I feel like I could tell him off a hundred times right now."

"Did you see the look on his face when you said you wanted tampons? Oh my God, Leslie, he was stunned." Monica started to giggle, trying to keep it under her breath, but it was contagious as I realized my victory. It felt good to stun him.

FAMILY PLOT

CATHERINE SPEARNAK

It was 1975. I was seventeen, with peroxide-blond hair that I colored myself. I rolled the bright-pink pills in my sweaty palm. They were the same color as the sunset over the brilliant Sacramento sky. But I hardly noticed. I had other things on my mind.

I was going to take these pills. They were only over-the-counter Sleep-Eze, but they might do what I was hoping. I had gotten a B in my English class. That was unacceptable. Unacceptable. To me, at least. I was used to getting nothing but an A. I didn't know anything about pills, but I was hoping I would float away on a pink pill cloud, so like the beautiful sunset.

I was parked in my parents green Falcon on School Hill, where everybody went to make out on Saturday night. Finally, I started taking the pinkies, drowning them one by one with Diet Coke. Soon I felt drowsy, and I had only taken about five pills. I was scared. I headed home, less than a mile away. I parked the car in the garage and walked in, where my mom was cooking in the kitchen.

I showed her the bottle.

"I took these," I said.

"What?!" she shouted. "All of them?!"

"No. Just five."

"Well thank God. Go in your room and lay down. Walt, go talk to your daughter."

You might think any normal mother would take her daughter to get her stomach pumped at the hospital. But no. Georgianna couldn't deal with that. She couldn't even talk to me. She put it on my dad.

"Walt, what are you doing?" she asked. "You know I can't deal with her."

"Okay, okay. What's going on?"

"Your daughter took some sleeping pills. Now go talk to her. She'll listen to you!"

I was seeing a therapist, but they didn't even think to call him.

"Cathy, you're going out to find a job tomorrow. That'll solve this."

I started crying, ran to my room, and locked the door. My dad knocked quietly.

"Cathy, let me in. Come on honey, let me in."

I just laid on the bed and cried. I stared at the orange and hot-pink shelves that my dad had built for me, the white blow-up chair, and the hot-pink and orange coverlet that I sunk into. Everything the same colors.

"Does she still have those pills?" Mom asked.

"I don't know," Dad said. "We've got to get in there. I think there's a utility key that opens all the doors in the house. Let me find it." He hustled off.

No one wanted to be around me. No one wanted to help me. What was wrong with me?

Dad came back with the key.

"Honey, give me those pills. Now just go to sleep."

I woke up about noon the next day to two parents who acted like nothing had happened. I walked to A&W and applied for a job. I got it. Kudos to me. Screw my parents.

PASSING

STEVE MONTGOMERY

"GO! C'MON, PUSSIES! NOW! C'MON, YOU PUSSIES! GET YOUR ASSES OFF THE GROUND! GO! GO! GO!"

Coach Otto's voice assaults every ache in my body, as if he is the master of a voice-operated torture device that implants malevolent clamps designed to squeeze every muscle I possess. I am going to pass out. I know, with certainty, that I am going to pass out. Only fear keeps me conscious. I feel a giant hand on the small of my back. The hand grabs and twists the waistbands of my athletic shorts and jock, twists them so hard that they become a vice in my crotch. I feel my eyes water. The hand yanks and my legs are airborne. I know what I am supposed to do. I begin crawling forward, using my forearms to propel me across the grass. I am a human wheelbarrow, sagging with fatigue. I wonder how I am able to put one arm in front of the other. I feel the dry Idaho sun on my neck. My body is soaked in sweat. Someone is shouting in my left ear.

"YOU ARE SUCH A PANSY, MONTGOMERY. C'MON, CRYBABY! YOU WANT YER MOMMY? MOVE IT!"

The hand lets go and I collapse on the fifty-yard line. The hand's owner steps over me and heads toward his next victim. Through blurry eyes, I see Coach Palmer's wide ass and hairy legs moving down the field. He spits Copenhagen every few yards.

It is a sweltering day in late August 1974. For reasons that have more to do with my father than with my desire to play football, I am an official member of the Alameda Junior High Yellow Jackets. Our ninth-grade squad is in week four of summer practices, and I do not understand why I am still alive.

Coach Palmer brings out the Scorpio in me. I fantasize about revenge. The more he humiliates me, the more elaborate my fantasies become. I imagine strapping him to a blocking dummy and letting the entire defensive line pummel him for hours. I picture myself collecting cups of brown spit from all the chew-boys and forcing Palmer to take a bath in Copenhagen. Best of all is the one where I get to scream obscenities at him while he suffers the agony of Yellow Jacket Road; in my fantasy he is always naked, causing him to earn grass burns in tender places.

Yellow Jacket Road is the invention of our head coach, Dick Otto, and he is always telling us that he designed The Road with one goal in mind: peak conditioning. Coach Otto always talks about conditioning, but he never seems to notice what condition I'm in. I am what is called a third-stringer, the name they give to those of us the school makes the coaches keep on the team, despite our total ineptitude on the field. It's the '70s, and the school is all about improving our self-esteem; no one is turned away. I am convinced that Coach Otto is sickened by the sight of me. He knows what I am, and it is only now, after years of therapy, that I understand who he was and why I made him squirm. On this hot August day, however, I am only aware of his disdain. Otto barely speaks to third-stringers. I am certain that he instructs his assistant coaches to make us so miserable that we quit the team. I am determined not to quit—I just don't understand why.

I dread Yellow Jacket Road every single day. We are divided into small groups along the fifty-yard line, stretching from one side of the field to the other. For what seems like an eternity but is really only ninety minutes, the coaches put us through a series of drills that I can only describe as physical and mental torture. Every drill requires us to move up five yards, back five yards, up ten yards, back ten yards, and so on, until we have run half the length of the field and back. At first we do basic sprints forward, backward, and sideways—one foot crossing over the other in a scissors pattern. But then we crawl on our hands and knees, or pull ourselves along by our forearms, dragging our legs behind us, or waddle like ducks until our legs feel like goalposts beneath us.

The physical pain is excruciating. The humiliation is worse. The coaches seem to believe that the worst insults they can spew at us are the ones that liken us to women or homosexuals. Favorite invectives of the first order include "girls" and "ladies," as in, "C'mon ladies, we're not puttin' on a goddamn fashion show. Put away yer girlie makeup and start playin' some FOOTBALL!" When it comes to the other category, each coach seems to have his favorite expression. Coach Otto's word of choice is "pussy" ("Yer all a bunch of pussies! That's what ya are! Pussy-boys!"), while Coach Palmer prefers "pansy" ("Montgomery, yer nothin' but a goddamn pansy!"). Coach Little, the lead offensive coach, is partial to "fairy," usually accompanied by an exaggerated mince-dance and what are still the limpest wrists I've ever seen (and believe me, I've seen plenty). Whenever he does this, I run a mini-movie in my head: the coaches are all at Otto's house drinking beer and watching Monday night football; their halftime entertainment features Coach Little doing his Little

Dance over and over and over, like a deranged monkey. It helps me get through practice.

"SHOWERS!" That thrilling word. That line of demarcation: practice is over. I have survived one more day. I suddenly feel a surge of energy, and I spring to my feet. I am surprised at my body's ability to do anything. Moments before, I was incapable of movement. Now, I am running across the field. It is the promise of the locker room, the cool-hot water, the permission to laugh, the absence of order. Boys allowed to be boys once again. Still, I am out of my element. This is the wide world of sports, and I have managed only a narrow point of entry. I am not a flipper of towels or a grabber of genitals. In the locker room, I become an anthropologist. I observe them—their unstudied movements, the jocular cadence of their speech, the way they put on underwear. These are the boys my father conjured during those joyous nine months of waiting, anticipating, longing. I was not in the picture.

So, I must learn the things that they know through instinct. Every moment I am in their presence is an education. My own fear of being discovered makes me uncharacteristically silent. The less I say, the more they will think I am one of them. Passing has become my pastime. It will be many years before I grasp the toll that passing requires. I am certain that it is my eyes that give me away. I cannot help but stare. I am surrounded by physical beauty made even more potent because I have earned the right to be there. Perhaps that is what propels me to follow the Yellow Jacket Road to its grueling conclusion. I may not be able to throw a ball or tackle an opponent, but I have not given up, and that should stand for something.

I reward myself with furtive glances. There is the sheer bulk of Karl Donaldson, taller and wider than every other boy, his muscles honed by moving irrigation pipe in the summer and harvesting potatoes in the fall. I am fascinated with the hair that covers every inch of Vince Farrelli. At sixteen—he's been "held back" twice—he has more body hair than anyone I've ever seen. Since I am practically hairless, to my eyes Vince is part movie-star sex symbol, part can't-turn-away-from-it circus freak. There is the fullness of Brett Ray's jockstrap. There are Lonnie King's ultra-broad shoulders. And there is the way Bobby Robertson's pale skin glistens when he's wet.

But my favorite is Randy Ford. He is perfect. Long brown hair that sticks to his neck when he sweats. Wide brown eyes with lashes you just want to lick. A mouth that pouts even when he smiles. And a body any sculptor would be proud to claim. Lately, I find myself conserving glances for him. I have worked out an elaborate algorithm in my head, and each day I allot myself so many "secret looks." My daily allotment tends to go up according to the misery level of that day's practice. The more I'm around Randy, the less I want to look at the others. I am so nervous around him that I can barely say hello, and I am constantly in fear that he will catch me staring at him. I am both embarrassed and exhilarated by my own boldness.

"What're you lookin' at, faggot?"

I am frozen. My ears begin to burn and I imagine that my face is as red as Zeke Miller's hair. There is a scuffle behind me. I turn around to find Ricky Culpepper on the ground, his hands over his face, kicking his legs in self-defense. Brett Ray is standing over him, fist poised, shouting a string of obscenities. It is not the first time Brett has reacted this way. I have managed to fly beneath his radar, but others have not been so lucky. Especially Ricky, with his delicate features and high voice. Ricky doesn't even try to pass. I'm relieved that it's not me, but I am ashamed at my relief. I'd like to record here that I stood up for Ricky, that I fought the good fight—but I cannot. On that day, Ricky was camouflage, and I was chameleon. Every pansy for himself.

Ricky was gone long before we played our first game. His family moved to Nampa, and I moved up on the radar screen. But somehow I managed to claim membership on our "perfect season" team, although I don't recall playing in a single game. If I did, it is now just a blur of missed opportunities. I played positions that I am still unable to describe in any detail: center and nose guard. I was clearly left of center, and like Cyrano, the only nose I felt was worth guarding was my own.

A poster appeared in my bedroom a week after our season ended. Dad couldn't wait to follow me to my room, to see my reaction to the balloons and streamers and butcher paper: "WAY TO GO STEVE! #60" There were signatures from cheerleaders, and cutesy expressions of congratulations strewn about the thing. Celebration of a sports hero—it was the closest we would come to living out his dream.

While nearly all of my perfect-season teammates went on to play high school football, it was the end of the road for me. Everything that team sports required me to repress found expression in music and theatre. Instead of cold metal bleachers, my father watched from red velvet chairs, as I performed on a playing field of my own choosing. We eventually came to a tacit understanding that his dreams of one day watching his son score the winning touchdown were as unrealistic as my dreams of one day watching my father star in a Broadway musical. An uneasy accord—no passing required.

TRUSTING FATHERS

SARAH VOSBURGH

These times evoke much of the anxiety of my youth. I find myself viscerally connected to old fears and comforts, the connections intertwined like rose and briar. So it is, each time I get in my daughter's Mini convertible and she pushes the button to peel back the ragtop. With an almost imperceptible lurch in my stomach, I'm sucked through a wormhole into another time of convertibles and benzene.

It was the spring of 1964 in Bloomfield, Connecticut. The sun was warm, but the wind whipping at my hair in Mom's old boat of a black convertible was biting, and my fear was intense and relentless. *This was how the president died. I'm gonna die in this car. Someone can shoot me.* In my six-year-old mind, it left me at the same risk. I was an anxious kid in anxious times. Sputnik, Bay of Pigs, Khrushchev. All discussed at the supper table. I listened and worried.

Mom was delighted with the warm sun that day when we left school where she taught and I learned. I helped her yank and snap into place behind the backseat the cumbersome white top that squeaked and groaned.

We lived in a lower-middle-class neighborhood of blue- and newly white-collar workers in what would now be called "starter homes." Starter homes of today are nowhere near as sturdy or appointed. Built-in shelves, closets, drawers, fireplaces, and TV alcoves, with detailed floor and crown moldings, hardwood floors, and partially finished basements with "rec rooms." I couldn't wait to be home and inside where a stray bullet couldn't get me.

Coming in the back door from the brightness of the day to the kitchen left me temporarily blinded, but I could smell ink, and I heard the whoosh-whoosh of the printing press from my father's basement print shop. My mother smelled it too and saw excitement dawning on my face.

My parents called me *Gremlin*—the ever-present foil that printers say is responsible when things go wrong. Such was my nickname when I hung around the shop that consumed most of our basement. I wanted to be near my dad. I knew how to stay out of the way and watch. Once in a while, I was afforded some acknowledgment or lesson, or the privilege to draw or practice lettering on the light table.

My mother knew the shop, near my dad, was where I always wanted to be. It fascinated me. At the supper table, my dad talked about printing jobs. They were important jobs because *my dad* did them. He talked about paper, ink, presses. I knew about Crane & Co., watermarks, chain laying, coatings, rag contents, craft paper, newsprint, and different smells of ink: some acrid, others flat and sweet like communion wine.

"Change your clothes and your shoes before you go downstairs," my mother warned. A few months before, I had slipped on the wooden stairs in my new slick-soled, sturdy leather "school shoes" and fallen through the railing to the concrete. The resulting concussion meant lots of vomiting and waking every two hours to touch my nose. I was still obsessively careful on those stairs.

Following her command, I hung up my school dress and changed into play clothes chosen from built-in drawers, and simple sneakers—my PF Flyers. They had rubber soles to prevent slipping, and their TV commercials promised to make me "run faster and jump higher." I washed my face and hands, remembered to push back my cuticles because that's what my dad did, and headed for the chilly basement.

The press in the shop was a behemoth smack in the middle, and were I not fascinated by it, its whooshes, smells, magic, then I'd have feared and run from it like I did the furnace only yards away. Basements are a collection of shadows and threats. Tiny casement windows allowed only slivers of light that caught dust motes. Damp cement walls and floors added to the sense of a dungeon. But my father was there.

The shop was not a place I could enter without invitation, but I loved to sit on the fourth tread of the dark stairs and bask in the warm glow from the door, even though I feared dust and spiders lurking. I could see my father silhouetted against the long side table where he bent over the silkscreen, his squeegee pulls interspersed between the whoosh-whoosh of the press churning out its assignment in automation. He was larger than life. Not terribly tall, he was somewhat roundish with full, wavy hair cut close and a broad stoic face. He had beautiful hands with long graceful fingers that drew my eye as I studied him.

I was on those sinister stairs for what seemed like an eternity, my behind getting chilled and tight from fears. On the press was a job that required a photographic "plate." I watched each leaf enter from the full tray as pristine as could be, then whoosh through the turns and switchbacks until it clicked into place against the metal pan at the end of the run, covered in **Garamond Bold**.

Maybe he'll let me set my name on the composing stick! I knew how to set a single line of type, use furniture for spaces, and keep track of letter placement from right to left.

My father was screening tonight too, working on the family Christmas card. He pulled, picked up the screen, took out his work, walked to the end of the line of other papers lying in ordered succession to dry, placed it, paced back to grab another leaf, placed that, laid the screen, pulled, and so on in an unrelenting and mesmerizing rhythm. His movements and steps were deliberate and sure. My breathing slowed to his methodical pace, though fears hardened in my cold and clenching. *There are always spiders down here. Can't get my PF Flyers dirty on the dusty stairs. The furnace is noisy! Does he know I'm here? Will he let me in tonight? Is it a work-alone night?*

As he cleaned the screen, the heady, sweet-sharp smell of benzene made its way to my stair before he turned to me and nodded. His signal, I was free to wander in. I stood next to him as he mixed ink for his next run, fascinated by the precision with which he matched and mated colors. The smells were so good, so familiar, that I could eat them, bathe in them, sleep with them covering me.

Later, we would learn that benzene was a carcinogen, but it's what we used to clean ink from our fingers, hands, and equipment. Once, my dad had a job printing periodic tables, and one of them was on the print shop wall. I knew where to find the benzene elements on that chart, and I knew it was a compound of carbon and hydrogen, equal parts. I understood the black carbon. The ethereal nature of hydrogen in the air all around me was a mystery.

The press behind me warmed some chill from my tightness. I turned to study it. It had its own secure rhythm, like my dad. It too churned out product precisely, perfectly, predictably. Dad noticed my interest. "Grem, want to hold your hand over the roller and see how hot it gets?" I nodded. I never touched anything in the print shop without invitation. My father was keenly aware of dangers to me, and he had made it clear that I would lose shop privileges if I violated his rules.

He lifted me because my PF Flyers wouldn't bring me up that far, even if I could have jumped higher. He demonstrated, holding his hand over the wet, glistening top roller. I carefully mimicked his motion, and he slapped my hand down, covering it with ink. I didn't have time for surprise and only barely registered what had happened before he said, "Never trust anyone, not even your own father," as he cleaned my hand with a ready rag soaked in my beloved benzene.

I struggled to raise my hand to my face to smell the ink. This annoyed him, and he admonished me to stay still. I wondered what I had done wrong to bring the stern voice. I was curious, but it didn't occur to me to ask for clarification or to be astonished or shocked. This was a lesson, and though I didn't understand, it would be my responsibility to divine meaning for the betterment of my life, because my father was wise and he imparted wisdom to me. But, in the moment, it was curiosity, bewilderment.

Afterward, he tied an apron around me which, despite folding and rolling, reached almost to the floor, and he allowed me to help lay the complete leaves for the second run of the Christmas cards. When the run was done, he cleaned the screen with rags and benzene. The room at rest and the lights off, he set me on the second stair, and I forced myself not to charge ahead, leaving basement bogeys because my father's protection was behind. The disparate smell of my mother's sweet, smooth, hot-spiced peaches wafted to the top of the stairs and greeted us as we blinked into the fluorescent brightness of the kitchen for supper.

My dad would leave presses and ink shortly after that, and we would move to a more affluent community. His company bought out, he gained executive positions in printing companies and came home with clean hands. I would miss those times when I sat next to him in church holding hands, inspecting stained pads and nails. I told him once I thought he was happier when he came home with dirty hands. To this day, when I work with various media and colors, I'm proud of the stains I carry for days.

Many were the frustrations and betrayals my dad experienced in life. I grew up thinking he had it worse than most. I came to understand he handled it worse. We all deal with disappointments and betrayals. His were discussed in living color, at the table, followed by the caveat, "Never trust anyone. Not even your own father." Were I to offer forth a story of my own disappointment or betrayal, it would be met with "Never trust anyone. Not even your own father."

It was early April in another spring, four months into my dad's retirement from the corporate world, and two weeks before he would leave my world. I stopped to see him at a print shop where he was helping. It was a retro place that still did typesetting and engraving. He gave me a tour, and I breathed deeply of paper, ink, sweat, heat, and oil. These smells are to me what baking bread or Sunday roast are to others. No beloved benzene, though. One of the presses was running, and he showed me the job it was completing. Then he said, "Hold your hand over the roller, feel how hot it gets."

SLAP! And suddenly, I was six again, standing in our basement, surprised, and happy with the smell of ink on my hands. In the now, my father growled at me, "I taught you better than that! Never trust anyone, not even your own father!" He helped me clean the ink from my hands with some thinner that didn't work near as well as benzene. At his funeral, I still had ink-stained hands.

Indeed you did teach me well, Dad. I'm not sure it was the lesson you intended, but you taught me well. You taught me you loved me, and you didn't want me to endure hurt and betrayal. You taught me you loved me and if you were able to protect me from hurt and betrayal, you would have done so with the slap of a wrist on a roller. And, by your example, because you always kept going back for more, you taught me it's worth it to keep loving, even when it hurts.

TAR BEACH

ILENE HUBBS

In the summer of 1957, my life began to change. I was graduating from junior high, our family was moving to a "better" neighborhood, and it was my first summer at my grandparents' new house at the Jersey shore. It was also the summer that *Bandstand* went national, soon to be renamed *American Bandstand. Bandstand* was a local dance show that featured high-school-age teens dancing to rock and roll, and it was my favorite TV show.

I raced home every day after school to be there in time for the start. Sitting on the sofa in our small living room, my after-school snacks at my side, I was always envious. I was dying to go on the show and dance. It filmed in Philly, just a short bus-and-subway ride from my home in Camden, New Jersey. I constantly pressured my mom to let me go. I knew every dancer's name. I knew that Justine was going steady with Bob, and Big Ro and Little Ro were cousins. I wanted to be friends with all of them.

Begging never worked well with my mom; no meant no. She said the kids who went on *Bandstand* were not like us. "Nice girls don't go on *Bandstand*." As years went by, I began to understand that to my mother, nice meant Jewish. And Jewish girls were expected to be different and to stick with our own. My mother's explanation of nice made no sense to me. Many of the dancers still had on their uniforms from Catholic school. *Aren't they the ultimate nice girls?* Mom stood her ground.

I didn't know until I was old enough to look back and compare, that the neighborhood I lived in was considered a poor, working-class area. It was all I knew. I never thought of the houses as shabby, but when I showed my husband where I grew up, he asked if we were poor. Most of the residents were working-class German and Irish, and everyone was some denomination of Christian.

Friday was payday. My parents knew that because the customers that ran up a tab all week would pay up after work on Friday. Summers, there seemed to be a lot of drinking on Friday nights, and we were often serenaded with some hard-core yelling coming out of the open windows. I think that might be why my mom got so crazy if we ever raised our voices in public. Maybe she thought that made us sound like, as she referred to our neighbors, "them." But I always knew we weren't like them. We were the Jews who owned the corner grocery store.

Living behind and above a grocery store was normal to me. Although there was a side door that went directly into our living room, I liked to get there by going through the front door of our store with the big bright neon sign outside proclaiming **Harry's Groceries**. Harry was my dad.

As soon as you entered, to the side, there was a big glass counter where an old-fashioned brass register sat. Behind the glass, all neatly arranged so the kids could clearly see each kind, was an inviting display of what was called "penny candy." There was everything from candy buttons and big red wax lips to tiny Tootsie Rolls and root beer barrels. After school, I was allowed to grab a few of my favorites as I made my way through our small store to the very back.

Behind the counter and through a tiny hallway was the door to my home. We only had a modest living room and kitchen on that floor, and in that living room sat our TV where I could watch *Bandstand*. Dick Clark was the new host now, ever since the original guy got caught with a fifteen-year-old uniform-clad girl who danced on the show. So much for "nice girls."

Growing up the only Jewish kids in our neighborhood, my siblings and I were used to our share of taunts at school. We were the Jewish merchants who let the customers buy food on credit. We were the Shylocks. I used to laugh to myself when some wiseass kid attacked me with, "You killed Christ" or simply "Christ killer." I wanted to shout, "I wasn't there! I wasn't even alive then!" But I knew, somewhere deep in my DNA, to just say nothing, not a word. It was safer.

When I got to junior high, I was no longer the only Jewish kid. That school pulled from more neighborhoods and now there were three of us. That's where I found a best friend. I thought Renee was beautiful and I loved her deep voice. She had thick straight black hair that made me hate my curls in comparison. We spent hours armed with curlers and hairspray doing each other's hair while listening to rock and roll records. I still know all the words to "Blueberry Hill" and "Sweet Little Sixteen." We read the same movie magazines and knew the importance of a perfect summer tan without strap marks. We argued over who was more in love with Paul Newman. We were bonded.

In the summer, we would change into our bathing suits and grab two towels each and the bottle of baby oil mixed with iodine. We knew the exact ratio of oil to iodine. It was all in the color blend.

The roof of the freestanding garage behind our house soon became our private beach. I loved climbing the steps to the roof, all sweaty and hot, to my version of paradise. Somehow, once on that roof, I felt cool again, as though I were stepping onto the sand at a real beach. We would spread our towels, double layers because the roof was tar paper and very hot, and when properly oiled, we would lie on our towels, plastic eye protectors on our eyes, and proceed with our tans. Lying there with eyes closed, I would imagine that we were on an exotic beach somewhere in California sunbathing with Paul and all his movie star friends, who were now our friends as well.

In August, my family was moving to a new, "better" neighborhood. I soon found that was Mom's way of saying there were Jewish people. It was the days when supermarkets were opening, and the mom-and-pop stores were all beginning to fail. Our store was one of them. My dad was going to work for a supermarket, and my mom was taking a secretary job. Money was tight, so our grandparents were helping us buy a house in an area, according to my mother, where kids would not taunt us. Our rooftop sunbathing was coming to an end. I had mixed feelings about moving. It was the only house I had ever known, and it was connected to a store stocked with candy.

But as good as the penny candy was, the neighborhood was starting to get to me. Just the previous year, I had been called out by one of the biggest bullies at my school. My chest had developed early, and one day after school, this mean girl, Bonnie Field—I will never forget her name—told everyone I stuffed my bra with paper. I was humiliated but stood up for myself, telling her "I do not stuff my bra." In front of all the kids, she came back at me with "then you have to prove it in gym in the locker room." Bravely, I told her I would not. She promptly "called me out" in front of my classmates. Calling out meant she challenged me to a fight.

For three days, I stayed home with a stomachache, some of it real, some of it feigned, until I finally told my mother the truth. I did not get the protective response I expected. "Go back to school and deal with it," she said.

I went through that school day knowing I had to face the music. What I faced was an orchestra of what looked like the entire school waiting to follow sturdy, buck-toothed Bonnie Field and pony-tailed, weak me over to the vacant lot nearby to watch us fight when school let out. I was small. I was scared. I had no choice. I put my two hands into what looked to me like menacing fists and stood my ground. I was no match for this amazon. She ducked my pathetic punches and proceeded to land several hard blows to my face and body. I ran crying and bleeding to a friend's house close by. The bully was vindicated and for some reason never bothered me again. I think if I ever saw her, even this many years later, I would punch her in the mouth. I am still small, but I am a lot tougher now.

Besides my first and only fistfight, that neighborhood holds other firsts for me. By junior high, I knew I was a bit boy crazy. I had played my fair share of kissing games at parties in grade school and "five-minute honeymoon" was my favorite. That's when I got to go into a closet with a boy and spend five minutes in there. Mainly, it consisted of feeling very self-conscious, and it usually ended with a fumbling attempt at a kiss on the lips. I liked it a lot. Chickie Slade must have sensed that when he pulled me behind the shed near St. Martin of Tours church and kissed me long and hard. Our mouths stayed closed, but the kiss lasted a good five seconds. I liked it. I also liked his name, "Chickie Slade." It sounded dangerous; Chickie was not a "nice" boy.

That summer I began to separate myself from that place. The lure of the rooftop beach was overshadowed by the anticipation of a real beach. Renee was soon to be replaced with girls from my new neighborhood. The excitement of a first boyfriend was yet to be experienced. The tar was turning to sand.

THE FISHERMAN

KRISTEN BALELO

It wasn't the first time I sat in this cold, stark cathedral, mourning the passing of a loved one. In the caramel-colored wooden pew of the church where I had been baptized and attended grade school, on the same grounds where my parents were married more than fifty years before, I watched the priest, in his cream and gold robes, prepare for the most sacred part of the mass.

Normally, he would have had an altar boy to bring him the water and wine, to hold the Bible while he recited the prayers, but it wasn't imperative. I let it go, bowed my head, and said a silent prayer for Aunt Beverly, for her family, for my family, and for myself.

"You're going to have to come out of retirement," I heard Uncle Will say in what he must have thought was a whisper. Sitting directly in front of me, he was leaning into the ear of one of his oldest friends, telling him, "They need an altar boy."

"Shhhhh!" His wife flicked him on the back as my nephew and I did everything we could to contain ourselves. I am certainly not the best Catholic, but at forty-three years old, I knew better than to laugh at a funeral. I had been chastised in this very church for laughing more times than I could count, by teachers, by nuns, and by my parents. And yet, I knew Aunt Beverly, whose life I was there to honor, who once widely smiled as she announced to a room full of people that I had become "awfully busty," wouldn't mind a little humor at her funeral.

Throughout the full cathedral sat people I had known my entire life: friends, relatives, and neighbors. But in my pew and the pews directly in front and behind me sat the people I loved the most. And yet, I barely recognized some of them, especially the men who sat in front of me. They were my father's cousins and his best friends, friends closer than most family. Now, deep into their seventies and eighties, they were old. They were gray, balding, wrinkled. But before they were old, they were fishermen.

They were all little boys in the 1940s, growing up together in Point Loma, a small suburb on the coast of San Diego. Back then, if you were raised in Point Loma, you were either a Portuguese immigrant or the child of one. These guys did everything together—first as playmates, then as schoolmates, and eventually as shipmates. Before any of them graduated high school, turned eighteen, or got married, they had spent significant time on commercial tuna-fishing boats. Their parents had flocked to coastal cities to pursue the American dream. Commercial fishing became their way of life, and they expected their sons to follow suit.

The guys weren't always working on the same boat, but many times they saw each other out at sea. While the men were out fishing, their girlfriends, who eventually became their wives, would see each other regularly; one fishing trip could last four months or more. The wives became best friends themselves, second mothers to me, and their children my playmates and closest friends. This community became family.

When my dad was home between fishing trips, my parents would host huge parties, especially after my parents moved out of Point Loma in 1980 and bought a sprawling ranch house in a more rural area. The fishermen would load their families into their cars and caravan the thirty minutes to our house, where we had almost an acre of land.

We kids would spend the day swimming, playing pool, hiking to the creek behind our house, riding Big Wheels down the long winding driveway, and roller skating around the tennis court. These are my most precious childhood memories. The women gossiped in the kitchen while the men congregated around the barbecue, drinking highballs and cooking hot dogs, hamburgers and *carne espeto*, the Portuguese version of shish kebob.

"Hey! *Compad*!"

"What do you say?" My dad's cousin, Uncle John, who never missed a party, would ask, a twinkle in his eye. He quit fishing as a young man after being hit in the head by a large cable. He was lucky. He never fished again, but it didn't matter. Theirs was a fraternity with perpetual membership. The fishermen would answer him with big smiles, hearty laughter, and a robust handshake, leaning into each other closely as they swung their left arms around their friend's neck.

"Not bad, not bad." The fishermen even have the same posture, their legs apart, just wider than shoulder width, hands clasped behind their back. It was as if they needed to ground themselves to the deck, bracing themselves for the wild swells of the sea.

"Bird! You had a good trip!" they would say, lifting their cocktails, toasting each other's good fortune, calling each of other by their nicknames. At well over six feet, Bird towered over the rest of the short Portuguese men. I still don't know if Bird's nickname referred to his tall stature or his larger-than-average nose; I really think it just depended on the day. Another of the fishermen was Buns; I was told it was because all of the girls thought he had a great *coo*.

Back in their day, San Diego was the hub of the commercial tuna-fishing industry. In the 1950s, '60s, and '70s, you would find downtown San Diego lined with the majestic commercial fishing boats docked along its piers. The massive purse seiners, sometimes 150 feet long, looked like magnificent yachts, grandiose and sleek with an imposing dark blue bow, the rest a modern, stark white.

I only remember watching my father's boats sail into the harbor a couple of times, mostly for repairs. By the time I was born, the local canneries had closed and moved overseas where it was cheaper to do business. When they were docked here, my father never let my brothers and me go on the boats, but Buns would let his boys spend time with him on his boats. I always felt jealous of how much fun they had spending that time with their dad.

"Your dad wouldn't let me bring any of you down to the boat," my mom said once. "He didn't want you to fall in love with it." At the time, I didn't understand. For generations, the tight-knit Portuguese community passed down everything from the old country; their language, their food, their traditions, their livelihoods. My brothers would have been expected to be fishermen, and me the wife of one. But that's not what my father wanted for us. That's not the life any of these men wanted for their children. They missed so much—birthdays and holidays, births and deaths, baptisms and weddings, first steps and graduations, and everything in between.

In the church parking lot, I heard the fishermen acknowledge each other with the same familiar greetings, calling each other by their nicknames. I watched the same intimate yet masculine embraces. But they weren't laughing or telling stories or drinking highballs today. Inside the church, as the fishermen recited the prayers memorized in their youth, they stood in the same fisherman stance, despite having retired from fishing years before. They knew, maybe now more than ever, that the sea still had the power to make them lose their footing.

I lost my footing more than twenty-five years ago, on the fourteenth of December 1990. I was seventeen years old when there was a knock on my parents' door at an ungodly hour, the owner of my dad's boat on the other side. No one had to tell my mom. She knew. My mother's screams and the footsteps of the fishermen's wives, running up the stairs to my bedroom, had alerted me that something was wrong. They told my little brothers and me about the accident. An explosion. A fire. The boat sunk. Four men missing.

They led me gently down the stairs, holding me tightly as I cried seeing my mother crumpled on the floor, supported on both sides of her by the fishermen. The ones who weren't there that morning came later that day. Each time one of them entered through the front door, our hearts broke over and over again. All of us sat in this same church back then, only it was my family sitting in the front pew. My father missed every single one of my adult milestones. While he couldn't be there, I always had Buns. And Bird. And Aunt Beverly. And all of the fishermen and all of their wives and all of their children. They have kept me alive, and they have kept my dad alive.

They have made me laugh with stories about how my dad was kicked out of every school he ever attended, how his Portuguese temper got him in trouble on more than a few occasions, how much he adored my mother, and how proud he was of my brothers and me. They have brought him to life. For that and for so much more, I am grateful. With each passing, I lose more of him. Their memories. Their stories. But most of all, I appreciate exactly what it was, or rather who it was, he fell in love in with.

WHERE'S THE HARM?

NANCY G. VILLALOBOS

I stared open-mouthed at my Peruvian mother-in-law, Rosa Tapia de Villalobos. She couldn't mean it. Once again, she had blindsided me with the kind of old wives' tale people in Lima took in with their mother's milk.

Rosa came every morning with fresh *granadillas* for my infant daughter, Rosalena, who shared the names of both her grandmothers. Rosa usually stayed a few minutes to chat and supervise the preparation of this gentle juice, which I had learned was the Peruvian infant's introduction to tropical fruit.

That day she had patted my daughter's head lovingly as the juice level went steadily down in the bottle, but something about the way she was avoiding eye contact had warned me that I, her American daughter-in-law, was in for another lesson in Peruvian child rearing. I was doing something wrong, or not doing something right, to my firstborn.

Shortly after her birth, I had been admonished to tie a red string around her tiny wrist to ward off *el mal ojo,* the evil eye, and to pin a small red bow to her sleeper for the same reason.

"The evil eye? What's the evil eye?" I'd asked, as visions of medieval sorcerers came to mind. Rosa explained to me about nefarious individuals who cast evil spells on infants by looking at them, causing sickness and even death. The terms *superstitious* and *uneducated* had popped into my head, but I was learning to mask my skepticism.

"I see."

"Of course, it's just something people believe," she said, carefully avoiding the word superstition. "But where's the harm?"

So Rosalena had worn the crimson protections while I took her for routine immunizations and followed the pediatrician's instructions for her diet and hygiene. Curiously enough, the doctor encouraged me to indulge the talismans.

"No, of course I don't believe in it," he had said. "But where's the harm?"

I gave it a month.

I was okay with that, but I refused to keep the windows closed at night to prevent *el mal aire* from entering the bedroom. Peruvians, I was learning, in addition to being terrified of cold beverages, were deathly afraid of breathing the night air. None of them would believe me when I mentioned that in the sorority house at IU, I slept in the Cold Dorm, without heat and with the windows wide open to the Indiana winter, without ever getting sick.

"Fresh air is healthy," I had insisted.

"Maybe over there, in the States (*where people are crazy*), but not here in Peru where everyone knows it's bad for you," they would say.

Still, in spite of my inexperience (but with the surreptitious help of Doctor Spock's *Baby and Child Care*), I was navigating this bicultural parenting thing and thought I was doing okay.

Until that day.

I watched as Rosa stroked the scant wisps of golden baby hair, lifting them gingerly and drawing them out into the air with her fingertips. There was something curiously akin to disdain on her face. I didn't have long to wait to find out why.

"*Pobrecita,*" she began. "Poor little thing."

I took a deep breath. I was still not used to Rosa's prefacing every remark about her granddaughter this way.

"Why do you say that? Why do you feel so sorry her?" I once asked. "She's tiny. She's perfect. Why does she need our pity?"

Without removing her gaze from the button nose and rosebud mouth of her namesake, Rosa sighed.

"Just think how much suffering she'll endure in her lifetime!"

The fatalism of that remark had left me speechless, and not only because I was learning to keep my opinions to myself. I also knew that it was entirely possible that at some time in the future I would come to comprehend, if not to share, Rosa's point of view. Just then, however, I didn't get it, but clearly something else was up.

"Just look at how thin her hair is, poor little thing." Rosa regarded me accusingly. The desirability of thick hair had never occurred to me. Fingers and toes, regular facial features, and other normal body parts constituted my requirements for a physically complete baby. I just assumed she would have serviceable hair.

"She's only eight months old," I reminded her. "It'll get thicker as it grows."

"No, it won't," said Rosa, firmly. "It will stay like this, all listless and pitiful, unless …. "

Unless what? I thought. My mind went to hair follicles, scalp tissue, genes—all things beyond my control. *What did she expect me to do?*

"Unless," she continued triumphantly, "you shave her head!"

My jaw dropped. She went on, nodding sagely, sensing a weak spot in my armor.

"That's right. Children's heads need to be shaved so the hair will grow back nice and thick. Like pruning trees. Hair is the same way. You shave it all off. It grows back thicker." And then, the kicker: "That's the way we do it here in Peru." She crossed her arms.

I recalled my own baby pictures with that same kind of blond hair that had turned darker and much thicker as I grew. I pictured my mother's head of beautifully dense silver hair. *Why did we have a problem?* Then I remembered that I had never known my father with more than a thin ginger fringe around the back of his head.

"You shaved your children's heads?" I asked. She nodded happily. "Just so the hair would grow in thick?" Big smile.

I shook my head. Her three children did, indeed, have lots of hair. But so did most Peruvians! All those Inca descendants had thick ropes of braids to their waists. And Spaniards, if you wanted to get anthropological, had had thick mats of dark (and possibly lice-infested) locks under those uncomfortable-looking conquistador helmets. *What's the big deal?*

"I'll think about it," I waffled.

Unconvinced, I confronted my husband, her son, about it later. In typical fashion, he ducked the issue.

"Where's the harm? It'll grow back. Either way. It's up to you. I don't care." He turned back to the soccer game.

Left in the position of either opposing or appeasing my mother-in-law, I decided to do some impartial research. I consulted friends. All the Peruvian women had shaved their children's heads, but none of the Americans had, even the ones married to Peruvians—and all their children had normal amounts of hair.

"How can you compare a child's head to a tree?" My friend Margaret shook her own head in disgust.

Recalling my university science classes, I cast about for an equitable solution that would prove me right once and for all and settle this ridiculous issue. At length, I came up with the scientific method.

Observation: Peruvians shave children's heads so their hair will grow in thicker (a patently ridiculous assertion).

Hypothesis: Shaving a child's head will make the hair grow back thicker.

Procedure:

At that point, it became distressingly clear that I would have to shave only ONE SIDE of my child's head to prove my point. If I had been worried that my beautiful baby would look funny bald, the thought of her half-shorn settled the matter. I caved.

After all, *where's the harm?*

I lost the battle but avoided a war with my wonderful mother-in-law. Somehow, Rosa and I reached an unspoken agreement about this. The other three grandchildren survived infancy without having their heads shaved, and they all grew luxuriant tresses, a point I may have mentioned in passing (at every possible opportunity) at family gatherings.

Years later, when they all graduated from high school in California, the only accolade my Peruvian American offspring shared in their high school yearbooks was—wait for it—*Best Hair.*

WOOD

DILIA WOOD

My mother knelt down and spoke to me in Spanish: "No digas nada a nadie." Then repeated it in English to make sure I understood: "Don't tell anyone." She often took me to obscure places around Washington, DC, near where I grew up. This time, a store located in the living room of a brick row home. She held my hand as we walked through ribbons of smoke from burning incense. Candles in glass jars, crucifixes, and figurines of Catholic saints surrounded the room like a labyrinth. A dark hand waved from behind a white curtain, signaling for us to enter where a man dressed like a Catholic priest waited for us.

He embraced my mother like an old friend and spoke only in Spanish, but faster than my mother usually spoke, making it difficult for me to understand. They prayed. He gave her a candle. No charge. Thanks to God. Fingers dipped into a bowl of holy water, and she genuflected before a statue of the Virgin Mary.

My mother had a way about her that was secretive, suspicious, and highly superstitious. The one time my sister opened an umbrella in the house, my mother's scream rattled the walls. I was the youngest in the family by seven years, and out of observation for consequences, I learned to dislike umbrellas and to never question my mother. She believed negative thoughts spoken aloud could manifest into reality—self-fulfilling prophecies you may not have intended. The power of positive thinking and deep meditative prayer seemed to be her solution for all of life's problems. At a very young age I decided to keep my thoughts to myself, because to say something negative in front of my mother could result in a smack upside the head.

Which is why, on the few occasions I tried to ask her, "What am I?" I stood out of arm's reach. It was the one question I heard most often growing up. Meeting someone for the first time, they'd observe my face and hair and inevitably ask, "What are you?" Every time it happened I wanted to answer, but I didn't know how. One part of me felt self-conscious, while another part wanted to believe it was innocent curiosity.

I was too brown to be black or white. My hair was too curly to set free, always tamed into two long braids, twisted with gumball click-clacks. My nose and lips were flat and full. No one had ever asked the question quite the way a freckle-faced kid did on the day we stood beneath a crabapple tree, waiting for the school bus. He did what cocky kids in the DC schoolyards used to say; he gritted on me. Looking me up, down, and up again before saying, "You don't look black, or Spanish, or white." Then he asked, "So, what are you?"

We stared at each other, waiting for my explanation. A tingling sensation on my face, neck, and chest left me feeling embarrassed for not having an answer either one of us could validate. I paused and pondered why I had to pick one and what difference it made. I considered pointing out his freckles to break the silence but had nothing more to offer except an awkward laugh and a deaf ear: "What?"

My sense of ethnic ambiguity was something I believed I had in common more with my father than my mother. A blue-eyed African American who, in his generation, according to the brown-paper-bag test, passed for "white." He was mixed—black, Native American, and white. He didn't speak or understand Spanish, and neither did I at the time. He was cool and calm, with contagious happiness that led me to believe he too was a positive thinker, but a natural one because I never saw him pray. Shopping at the G.C. Murphy's, I admired how he carried on pleasant conversations with strangers, including the lady with a blond beehive behind the cash register. As she placed my father's change in his hand, she looked down at me and said, "What do you want, little girl? You can't butt in line."

My father pulled me closer to him, dropped the smile from his face, and said to the woman, "She's with me." He rolled his eyes and we walked out, but I didn't grasp why their pleasantries faded.

I often wondered if my father was ever asked, "What are you?" I wanted to ask him, but I waited too long. Twenty-eight days after my twelfth birthday, he fell to one knee in our living room. As he reached for the velvet sofa with one hand he clawed at his chest with the other, his blue eyes jammed wide open as if to beg me not to watch as he passed away from a massive heart attack. The smell of his cologne—Old Spice—lingered with a hint of vanilla that reminded me of the French toast he'd make on Sunday mornings. I wanted to hold him but was rushed to my room and out of the way as the commotion to call an ambulance broke loose. My body trembled and shook before a tear ever surfaced, and I shivered on the floor, listening beneath the crack of my door. Sirens. Wailing cries. The essence of vanilla and a clackety gurney rolling out the front door.

It felt as if almost everything that gave me a glimpse into a sense of who I was had left. My older brother and sister had moved out on their own, and it was just my mom and me. She spent more time at church and in prayer than she had done my whole life before. My father's voice still rang in my ears with family stories I'd eavesdropped on when his sister and cousins used to visit. Our last name, Wood, was not the name of the slave master. Great-great-great grandfather Oscar Bird Wood was said to be a house slave in the 1800s. The day he was emancipated, he walked alone down a dirt road where a fallen tree blocked his path. Climbing over the wood and beyond whatever else might block his way, he kept going and took the name.

My parents came from a generation forced to accept discrimination and racism until the Civil Rights movement of the 1960s. In the 1970s, when I was growing up, times had changed. Washington, DC, was known as the Melting Pot Capital of the World. An ideology of a color-blind society was being explored, and from my experiences, the notion of racism seemed passé, faux pas, and a sport for the ignorant. The difference from my parents' generation to mine was a meaningful perspective I imagined my father most likely experienced from his life in Washington, DC. I wondered how my understanding of the world would have been different had he still been with us.

By my freshman year in high school, I could no longer avoid the question. Kids and adults were asking, and the frequency grew from verbal to forms and applications with checkboxes. *Which classification best described me?* "Other" was never an option.

The moment I felt brave enough to push the question with my mother, she was standing at the kitchen counter, scraping the meat of a coconut with a seashell. The same seashell she brought from the fishing village in Ecuador where she grew up. I watched as she squeezed the milk from the coconut shavings with her bare hands and I wondered, *if she knew the answer all along, why had she never told me?* Taking deep breaths as I tried to convince myself that I wouldn't leave without an answer, I cleared my throat and asked, "Ma, what am I?"

She placed the seashell on the cutting board and allowed her broken English to sharpen as she spoke with a directness I didn't expect. "You are whatever you want to be, and don't let anyone tell you different."

I pushed the question further because I wanted to be an either/or like my friends, and by now I had a rainbow of friends—white, black, Indian, Korean, Pakistani—and still, everyone seemed to be able to identify as something, except me. They belonged to traditions and customs, lived without confusion, and carried an absolute clarity of who and what they were in the world.

"Well then, I must be black," I said.

"No. You are your own individual."

My efforts of being an individual in the past had only amplified the confusion. Spanish, mixed, multicultural, a bit of this, and a bit of that, and for each answer came more questions. Other people's confusion didn't seem to matter to my mother, so I pushed again: "Why can't I pick?"

"Because the color of our skin is not who we are. The outside world will try to convince you that you're nothing more than a color, or not as good as some other colors, and those are lies. You are the same as everyone else regardless of the color of your skin, and you can do anything you put your mind to."

How am I going to explain that?

She prayed for me.

At age forty-nine, I now know that my mother wasn't denying me a sense of identity. She was protecting me from inheriting a system of false beliefs and preconceived limitations imposed long ago for the sake of diminishing and dividing people.

I sometimes still ponder when a stranger asks me, "What are you?" I tell them the truth. I'm a daughter, a sister, a mother. An entrepreneur. A creative spirit, and someone looking for a better world, just like them.

SUNNY CAB

TRACY J. JONES

I need a fucking cab. God, please send a fucking cab down this ruined street. Cab. Cab. Cab. That was all my brain could process. It was only a few months after 9/11 and I was standing in the freezing rain on the corner of Greenwich Street and Rector in downtown Manhattan.

My new apartment was only one block away from the burning hole that was the World Trade Center. I had recently moved to the neighborhood, and it felt like living in a ghost town. Almost every store window was boarded up with plywood. No restaurants, coffee shops, or bars were open for at least five blocks. There was a constant burning chemical smell in the air that soon caused me to have nosebleeds every time I sneezed.

The inconvenience of living downtown was nothing compared to the heartbreaking daily reminders of all who were lost. Months after that horrible day, my neighborhood was still plastered with homemade flyers searching for loved ones. There was hope in those flyers. *Please call if you see Gretchen. She works at Cantor Fitzgerald and we can't find her.*

They showed happy faces at graduations, weddings, and barbecues. I had tried to forget that the ever-present dust—now mud in the pelting rain—was part of those lost souls, but it was impossible. Living downtown sickened me.

I had moved downtown as part of the Mayor's redevelopment plan. In exchange for venturing downtown, I had received a two-year grant that paid six hundred dollars a month toward my rent. My beautiful apartment had a sparkling gym and an in-house drycleaner and boasted ten of the nicest—but nosiest—doormen I would ever encounter.

Doorman Michael and I had had an uncomfortable encounter the day before, when I had to put my beloved cat, Sunny, to sleep. Sunny was only a pet, and my loss was nothing compared to what so many in the city were dealing with in the aftermath of 9/11, but it still hurt. I had convinced myself that Sunny's death was somehow my fault. I was profiting by living near a hallowed graveyard, and Sunny's death was the price I had to pay for a beautiful downtown apartment I couldn't afford without the grant. Death had now invaded my home like the dust that filtered through my open windows.

Having returned from the vet, I decided to burn sage in the apartment and "smudge" the death away. I lit a brightly tied bunch of dried sage and walked around my apartment, offering prayers for my neighborhood's lost souls and for the soul of my sweet cat. Deep in thought, I didn't notice when the burning sage erupted in billowing smoke.

Before I knew it, a fire alarm went off in my apartment, followed by alarms throughout the thirty-story building. Next came frantic knocking and Doorman Michael yelling, "Are you okay? We called the fire department!"

"I am smudging!" I yelled over the deafening alarms. "My cat just died. I am burning sage. It's a Native American thing. This is all for my cat!"

The next day, I added an even newer embarrassing moment with Doorman Michael. "You have a package from your gentleman friend." This was our inside joke because my boyfriend, Nick, was no gentleman. He was twenty years older, twice divorced, and a limo driver. I would later learn that he was also a part-time pimp. I simply thought he was a sexy distraction.

I opened Nick's brown bag and pulled out its contents on Michael's concierge desk. It contained a box of extra-large condoms, a half-empty bottle of Chivas Regal Scotch whisky, and a small bag of marijuana. Michael cleared his throat and began awkwardly shuffling the papers on his desk. Without a word, I scooped up the contraband and headed upstairs. I was beyond consoling over Sunny's death. *Maybe a little herbal remedy was just what I needed?*

Back in my apartment, a plan began to form. I needed a pipe to smoke that pot, and I needed a cab to get me somewhere I could buy one. I hadn't smoked pot in more than a year … not since my ex-husband had moved out. He had taken few items when he left: mostly clothes, books, CDs, his writing journals—and our pot delivery service number off the fridge. Now, with pot in hand, all I needed was to find a cab, in post-9/11 downtown Manhattan, on a Friday night in the rain. This wasn't going to be easy.

I raced downstairs and flew out the door of my building. I frantically scanned the street, never more alert for the lights of coming cabs. My mantra was simple. *CAB … CAB … CAB.* I began bartering with God. *I know you don't approve. But, just this one last time, I need to smoke. God, please send me a cab.*

After forty minutes of pacing and bargaining, I saw a cab in the distance with its ON DUTY sign glowing like a lighthouse beacon. As I began running and waving, I saw a Wall Street-type dart from under a doorway and hail the same cab. ***My cab***.

"Back off, motherfucker!" I yelled at the top of my lungs. I then blew right past him, opened the door, and entered the sanctuary of the cab's backseat.

In the quiet of the cab, with Mr. Wall Street still glaring, I cried out, "Drive! Just DRIVE!"

I saw that the driver was a Sikh with a twisted handlebar mustache and a light-blue turban.

"My cat just died!"

He stared back blankly.

"My friend just dropped off pot and I need a pipe. You need to drive me to a smoke shop so I can get a pipe."

Nothing.

"Pot. I need to smoke pot. You are supposed to know where things are. I am having a fucking bad day here. Can't you help me out?"

Silence.

He then cleared his throat and politely asked, "Do you have any suggestions, Miss, on where we should go?"

"You must be the only cabbie in the city that doesn't know where a head shop is!" Nick, my limo-driving boyfriend, had told me that every driver knew how to get girls, drugs, or whatever a client needed.

"Just go to the village!" I cried, beyond frustrated.

"East or Greenwich?" he calmly asked.

And that did it. I began to laugh. At first, it was mixed with ugly crying but soon it was just straight-up belly laughter. He started giggling and before I knew it, we were both in hysterics. And for the next two hours, we drove through the rain and traffic, searching for a Greenwich Village smoke shop. He was sweet and clueless about pot and smoke shops. We became a team together.

"No … there is a school on this street. They wouldn't allow it near children, right?" he helpfully asked.

"You're right! How about driving further east?"

"This street has too many fancy restaurants."

"I agree. We need a seedier section." He was kind and asked about my cat. I told him all about Sunny, my divorce, and Nick.

"There! It is there?"

"Yes, that's one! You did it! Pull over! Pull over!"

We high-fived, celebrating as if we'd won the lottery. I asked if he would wait. He smiled, turned off the cab's meter, and said, "Take your time." I ran in and bought the first pipe I saw. I was back in the comforting safety of his cab within two minutes.

"Where to now?"

"Home."

I don't remember much of the ride home. I started drinking the Chivas Regal in the backseat. We talked about everything and nothing. He was lonely. I was lonely. He missed home. I felt that since the divorce I no longer had a home or real place in the world.

Back in my apartment, $105 poorer, I got properly drunk and thoroughly stoned. It didn't make me feel any better about my life. The only healing I felt came from that turbaned cab driver. It came from being listened to. It came from hearing that someone else was lonely and disappointed by life. It was the most expensive cab ride I ever took, and it was worth every penny.

ACKNOWLEDGMENTS

Thank you to all of our writers, actors, writing coaches, judges, donors, sponsors, and volunteers and with special thanks to: San Diego Writers, Ink, Kristen Fogle, Kim Keeline, San Diego Memoir Writers Association, Jeniffer Thompson, Jocelyn Hough, Judy Reeves, Lindsey Salatka, Anastasia Zadeik, Brian Joyner, Rebecca Chamaa, Melissa Bloom, Jill G. Hall, Danielle B. Baldwin, Carlos de los Rios, Julia Alicia, Chad Thompson, Will Cooper, Jennifer Coburn, Tricia van Dockum, Kathy Bostrom, Karen Malfara, and Shiloh Rasmussen.

ABOUT THE EDITORS

MARNI FREEDMAN

Marni Freedman (BFA, LMFT) is a produced, published, and award-winning writer. After graduating from USC, Marni began her career with her play, *Two Goldsteins on Acid*, produced in LA. She worked as a script doctor and script agent. Her play was made into a film, *Playing Mona Lisa*, produced by Disney. Marni teaches at San Diego Writers, Ink, UCSD Extension, runs the San Diego Writers Network, and produces the San Diego Memoir Showcase, a yearly production that transforms written memoir pieces into compelling theater. Marni is also a therapist for artists and writers. Her welcoming, easy-going nature and solid background are the underpinnings of what makes her such a popular writing coach. Her first book, *7 Essential Writing Tools: That Will Absolutely Make Your Writing Better (And Enliven the Soul)* is an Amazon Bestseller. Marni recently co-authored a play, *A Jewish Joke*, about a 1950s comedy writer facing the Hollywood Blacklist; it won the New York Solo Show for best drama and was the Union Tribune's critics' choice. *A Jewish Joke* will be heading Off-Broadway in January 2019. Her next book, *Permission to Roar: For Female Thought Leaders Ready to Write Their Book*, will be published in September 2018. This year, Marni and Jeniffer Thompson are launching the first annual San Diego Writers Festival in conjunction with the San Diego Public Library on April 13, 2019. You can find Marni at www.marnifreedman.com or at thefeistywriter.com, a writing hub to help writers find their authentic voice.

TRACY J. JONES

Tracy J. Jones is a professional content writer and editor, ghostwriter, and copy editor with more than 25-years experience writing and editing for private clients, non-profits, and corporations including time as an executive speechwriter for companies such as KPMG LLP, the New York Times, and Avon Products, Inc. Tracy is the content editor and a featured writer at thefeistywriter.com. She's a producer, head judge, writing coach, and co-director of the annual San Diego Memoir Showcase. Tracy is the co-editor for the inaugural edition of the Memoir Showcase anthology, *Shaking the Tree*. She's a writing coach for SDWI's Certificate in Memoir Writing, a board member of the San Diego Memoir Writers Association, volunteer manager and programming support for the inaugural San Diego Writer's Festival, and has been a featured writer/performer in So Say We All's V.A.M.P. showcase. Tracy also runs three successful read and critique groups; one for memoirists at San Diego Writers, Ink on Saturdays, Tuesdays at Oasis San Diego, and another on Tuesday nights in La Jolla. She's currently turning her screenplay, *Don't Call Me Kitty!*, into a YA novel and plans to publish her memoir, *Starting Over at Ground Zero*, in 2019. For more information, email Tracy at tjjones1@gmail.com.